Over My Shoulder

Over My Shoulder

Ella White Robinson

Review and Herald Publishing Association
Washington, D.C. 20012

Copyright © 1982 by
Review and Herald Publishing Association

Editor: Bobbie Jane Van Dolson
Cover Design: Kaaren Kinzer
Cover Illustration: Bobbi Tull

Library of Congress Cataloging in Publication Data

Robinson, Ella May White, 1882-1977
  Over my shoulder.

  1. Robinson, Ella May White, 1882-1977. 2. Seventh-
day Adventists—United States—Biography. I. Title
BX6193.R62A36   1982   286.7′3   82-9060
ISBN 0-8280-0129-4   AACR2

Printed in U.S.A.

DEDICATION

While ever seeking wisdom from their heavenly Parent, our father and mother, Dores and Ella Robinson, at the same time poured into our upbringing their own unique brand of love, humor, comradeship, and compassion mingled with firmness.

To their memory we dedicate this book.

Virgil Robinson
Mabel Robinson Miller
Gladys Robinson Kubrock

Contents

BEFORE YOU BEGIN—

When Ella White Robinson was well along in years, she finally had time to look back over her shoulder, so to speak, and describe for us the panorama of her life. Her earliest memories take us back to the year 1885, when she was 3 years old and living with her parents, William C. and Mary Kelsey White, in Oakland, California. Her father divided his time between assisting his mother in her travels and the publishing of her books. He was also involved in the publishing and educational interests of the church on the West Coast. Her grandmother, Ellen G. White, 57 years of age and a widow, was residing in Healdsburg, about seventy-five miles to the north.

Then came an urgent request for Ellen White to visit and work in Europe, and also for her son William, then 30 years of age, to accompany her. His counsel was needed by the workers in Basel, Switzerland, who were just completing and furnishing a new publishing house in that country.

On August 7, 1885, the group sailed for Europe, returning to America two years later.

So now, let us begin to trace with Ella her memories, which will carry us back nearly a century to the years of her earliest childhood.

To a Far Country

As I trotted along beside the high board garden fence, trying to catch a butterfly that had no intention of being caught, I became aware of someone on the other side.

"Ella," called a little girl's voice, "can you come over and play with me?" It was Beth, my little neighbor.

"I can't," I replied, peering through the slats. "My mamma won't let me. You come over to my house."

"No, my mamma won't let me come to your house today."

Realizing that it was no use trying to have those profound decisions reversed, we settled down to make the best of a bad situation and carry on our play without actually being together—a difficult undertaking even for two imaginative children. Fortunately there was a fairly large knothole in the fence low enough for us to peek through, so we brought our dolls and attempted to conduct our routine game of playing house. We visited and shopped and, most important of all, disciplined our obstreperous children, singing them to sleep, petting them when they were good, and spanking them when they were bad.

Neither of us had a fancy doll. My Katheryn was only a poor raggie, stuffed with sawdust. Friends of the family had given me a beautiful doll, but Mother said that Angelina didn't have good health, and so I was not allowed to take her outdoors. Beth's one child boasted a china head. Since both of our "babies" were larger than the knothole, we were not able to exchange them. In spite of these difficulties, we had a wonderful time, as only 3-year-olds can.

One day I invited Beth to come to my wedding. Before my third birthday I had attended, with my parents, three weddings at the Pacific Press Publishing House in Oakland, where my father and mother were both employed.

"We had the nicest parties that I ever went to," I told Beth. "And I'm going to have one all my own, and I want you to come."

"Yes, I'll come if my mamma will let me. Will it be a picnic party?"

"No, it will be a wedding party. They're the nicest kind. I'm going to marry Bobbie, the boy that lives up the street. My mother knows how to make nice parties. She'll help me."

Disappointment! My wedding never came off, probably because of a lack of cooperation on the part of our parents. Soon great changes came into our home, and Beth and I lost track of each other. For days our house was the scene of intense activity—dressmaking, packing trunks and suitcases, farewell visits, then a long ride with Father, Mother, and Grandma White on the train. Grandpa James White had died in 1881, the year before I was born.

I don't remember much of that journey from California to Battle Creek and on to the East Coast, for I was only 3½ years old. But I do remember how it hurt when a cinder flew into my eye as I looked out the train window. I also remember climbing up the gangplank to the steamship *Cephalonia* in Boston. It looked enormous to me. On it we took a boat ride that lasted ten days. I recall a woman on board fed me soda crackers and broth. During the trip Mamma was terribly seasick and spent much time in bed. But Papa and I had a marvelous time looking at the engines and the other interesting things on the ship. One day I saw a whale that I insisted was "a mile long," because "Didn't I see its head way over there and its tail way, way over there?"

As all things do, the voyage came to an end. And we continued on by train. My next vivid recollection is of standing in a large room in a noisy building, clutching my mother's hand. Machinery roared all around us, and people spoke a language I did not understand. We were in the pressroom of the Imprimerie Polyglotte—the multilanguage printing office—in Basel, Switzerland, and Elder B. L. Whitney was showing our party through the building. He called for the pressmen to stop operations; then two young men came forward, bowing and smiling their welcome.

"I have seen this press before," said Grandma, looking around the room. "This room looks very familiar to me. But where is the other worker? There is an older man who works in this office, and I have a message from the Lord for him."

"Oh, that must be Brother Albert Deichy," said Elder Whitney, a bit surprised. "He is in the city on business today. You'll see him tomorrow." Grandma did see him the next day and delivered to him the message that God had given her in a vision in Battle Creek, Michigan, ten years before. Both Father and Grandma had often wondered when she would actually see those young men and the presses that God had shown to her so vividly. Here in Basel she saw the machines and talked with the same men, and she noticed that one member of the group, the older man, was missing.

Besides Father, Mother, Grandma and me, our traveling party included Sara McEnterfer, Grandma's secretary and traveling companion; Marian Davis, her literary assistant; and Christina Dahl, our cook and housekeeper. Miss McEnterfer was to be with Grandma for thirty-three years. To us she was always Auntie Sara.

The Basel printing establishment was in a new, four-story building that also furnished living apartments for the few mission families, as well as for those who worked in the press. Father, Mother, and I were soon settled in an apartment next to Grandma's.

Father and Grandma were away from home much of the time, traveling throughout the countries in Europe, visiting the scattered Sabbathkeeping churches and seeking to encourage the few ministers who were laboring to build a firm foundation of Bible truth on that continent. Grandma's sermons were unique and so powerful that she was sometimes asked to speak in the large popular churches and in public halls. On such occasions she usually chose as her theme "Christian Temperance" or "The Christian Home" or, very often, "The Love of God as Revealed in the Plan of Salvation." She became accustomed to speaking with an interpreter. I can remember seeing her standing before a multilingual audience in the auditorium of the printing office, where our Sabbath meetings were held. A little man, no taller than she stood by her side, and as she spoke a sentence in English, he would repeat it in French. Then it would be relayed to a group in German in yet another part of the room.

It was just outside this assembly room that Father administered to me the first spanking of which I have any memory. I had promised to be very quiet if permitted to play in a corner during a committee meeting.

But, forgetful, I dumped my box of small stone building blocks, clittery-clattery on the tile floor. My tears were copious, but they abated when I was finally able to grasp the fact that punishment was necessary to help me remember never again to be noisy during a meeting.

One Sabbath afternoon Mother and I went for a walk with some of the mission workers to inspect a cave said to be the home of a "petrified monk." The cave reverberated with moans and groans whenever the shabbily-dressed wooden figure held out his hand for a gift. With childlike curiosity, I slipped in behind the scene and saw a decidedly unpetrified man turning a crank to extend the hand.

"Oh, Mamma, they're fooling everybody," I blurted out.

"No, dear, they're really not fooling anybody. It's just a game they're playing," she said, trying to hush me up.

The mission workers usually spent Sabbath afternoons in the homes of church members, helping them find Bible answers to their many questions. Generally my parents took me with them on such visits, and often we were invited to dinner. I always closed my eyes and bowed my head when the blessing was asked. But I soon learned to give thanks again to God at the close of the meal.

One day Sister Whitney and her two little girls, Jean and Lenna, had an errand with the dressmaker, who lived a few doors from the mission. It was a pleasant afternoon, and she asked Mother and me to accompany them. Someone living at the home owned a little dog and a pet fox about 6 months old. We three girls went into the field back of the house to watch the fox and dog perform. They were chained together and were romping playfully. Jean held the chain while we stood in a circle watching their antics. Suddenly the fox darted at me and knocked me over. His mouth was open, and his lower teeth split my upper lip, and his upper teeth made an ugly gash above my left temple. Mother picked me up and quickly carried me home.

Someone was sent to call a doctor at once, but it was Sunday and none could be found. While waiting, Mother applied hot fomentations and stopped the bleeding. Then, without further ado, she cleaned the wounds, drew the split lip together and fastened it with court plaster (something like adhesive tape).

Mother put me to bed with a prayer of thanksgiving that the accident had been no more serious. Within three weeks the wounds were healed, but I carried the scars for eight years.

One morning a few weeks before my fifth birthday I was taken to Mother's room. She was in bed, and when I entered she turned back the sheet and showed me a tiny, pink baby doll that was alive and all our own. Auntie Sara McEnterfer, who was filling the role of family nurse, told me that the doctor had brought the baby in his satchel, which enlightening bit of information left me for years under the impression that Mabel was an adopted sister. Auntie Sara was young and had been with Grandma's family only four years. She had not yet learned that Grandma did not approve of such fabrications.

One night when Father was away from home Mother woke me in the middle of the night. "Run to the kitchen quickly and get a crust for Mabel to nibble on while her bottle is heating," she said. "Her crying will waken everybody on the floor." I slid out of bed and timidly started down the long, dark hallway. As I passed Grandma's room I saw a light shining out from under her door, and all my fear vanished. I knew she was just a few feet from me, wide awake and busy with her writing. It must have been sometime between two and four in the morning, for that was the time she usually began her day's work.

For my fifth birthday Grandma gave me a large, beautiful picture album. Inside was a package of colored pictures waiting to be cut apart and pasted in. I spent many delightful hours filling my album with lovely scenes of lakes and mountains, flowers and birds.

When my mother was a girl working at the Pacific Press in Oakland, she had learned shorthand by correspondence. Now she was able to take down Grandma's sermons in shorthand and then write them out.

While we were at the Basel printing office a class was begun in speaking and writing French, and Mother joined it and worked with the translator in getting Gramdma's sermons into tract form for circulation. When help was short, as it usually was, Mother would take it upon herself to set the type, also. This helped her make more rapid progress in learning the French language. With so much important work to be done and few people to do it, Mother was always busy. Little did any of us realize that she was setting the stage for tragedy, for the long hours broke her health and cut her lifework short.

With everyone busy I was often left in the care of Christina, our cook. One of my chief delights was to watch until she was absorbed in some kitchen task; then I would slip out into the hall and tiptoe along until I came to Grandma's door, where I would knock. At her invitation I would enter and stand quietly by her side until she laid down her pen.

That was her signal for one of those delightful visits I enjoyed so much. She would tell about her childhood—her twin sister, Elizabeth, her big brother, Robert, or perhaps about her pets. Sometimes she described children she had seen on her many train travels. She was too busy writing to visit long with me, so after a short chat, she would hand me a pair of small, blunt scissors and some pictures she had saved out of a magazine. I would sit on a footstool at her side and cut around the edges carefully as she had shown me.

When she saw I was getting tired she would hand me an apple or a peppermint and tell me to give it to Christina to put away till dinnertime. One day she said, "When you have done this, come back and we will go for a walk around the block." That day we ventured too far and got lost. Not being acquainted with the city and not speaking French, German, or Italian, we were a long time finding our way home and were late for dinner.

For two years Mother, Mabel (my little sister), and I lived at the Basel printing office, while Father and Grandmother, accompanied by Miss McEnterfer, traveled through Europe. They encouraged and counseled the workers and helped them organize churches and establish mission centers. About this time Mother became ill, and when baby Mabel was 5 months old all of our party except Father returned to America. He was detained for a time in Europe by council and committee meetings.

The activities of the return voyage are nearly a blank in my mind, except for the fact that my childish heart felt responsible for the safety of the vessel and its passengers. The sea was rough, and at times the ship rolled heavily. If this happened while I was on the lower side of the deck, I would hasten with all speed to the upper side with the conviction that my weight would help to balance the steamer. Then in another two or three minutes I would be running frantically back. This went on for hours. My efforts to prevent the vessel's capsizing proved successful, and the *City of Rome* finally entered New York Harbor right side up.

A Heavy Loss

We returned to America in August of 1887. Grandma began traveling immediately, for she was eager to attend as many of the summer camp meetings as possible.

My mother was not well. Her long hours of labor in the Basel printing office and her failure to take sufficient rest had drained her strength. She had developed a persistent cough that continued to grow more and more severe. Tuberculosis was suspected. It was evident that no time should be lost in getting her to the Battle Creek Sanitarium in the hope that she might be treated for that dread disease, which was generally considered incurable.

After Mother's examination Dr. John Kellogg made no comment. There could be no question about her having tuberculosis. However, he reminded us of Grandmother's statement regarding sunshine, fresh air, and outdoor living. Sunshine! Was not California the land of sunshine? So after a short period of rest and treatment at the Sanitarium, Mother hurried to the Far West, where she would receive good medical care and could take treatments every day.

In California, Mother and I spent much time together outdoors. She would rest and read, enjoying the fragrance of the evergreen trees that covered the hillside, while I gathered Johnny-jump-ups and ferns in company with little Milton St. John, one year my senior. Where baby Mabel was at that time, I do not know—probably in the care of some relative. I only remember that in those unsettled days I could list nearly a dozen aunties and cousins and grandmas who cared for Mabel and me at one time or another.

But what was it we were hearing about Burrough Valley, a prospective health resort north and east of Fresno in Central California? At the invitation of friends, Father and Grandmother visited this much-renowned place and found a few Adventist families living there.

They were enthusiastic in recommending it as a quiet resting place for invalids wishing to regain their health.

With borrowed furniture and dishes, Father helped Mother and Auntie McComber, her nurse, set up camp in a cottage in a retired spot. Grandmother secured the use of a pony and saddle for Mother, and Father invested a few dollars in a pony for me. Then, leaving us among friends, they hastened on to answer the call of duty and returned to their work. Daisy and Dixie, our mounts, took us for many a ride over the hills surrounding our little cottage, and Auntie McComber always had a good dinner for us when we returned at noon.

When tired of riding, Mother would spread a blanket in some shady spot and read and rest, while I luxuriated nearby, burying my feet in the cool, moist sand of a dry riverbed or digging tunnels and building castles in partnership with Beulah, a little girl four years my senior. Possessed of a strong supervisor complex, Beulah set herself the duty of disciplining me in obedience. How I longed and sighed for the time to come when I should be "grown up" like Beulah! Then, oh, then! But in spite of it all, I loved her, and we had good times together. Burrough Valley made rugged children of us little girls, but did little to help Mother. It was too hot there, and the idea of making it a health resort was abandoned.

In her recent travels among the churches, Grandma had visited Healdsburg, the town where she once lived and where, in 1882, our second Seventh-day Adventist College had been established. On the outskirts of town she found an old but roomy house with a flourishing fruit orchard attached, a berry patch, a windmill, several sheds, a farm wagon, harness and carriage, kitchen garden, and even some beehives. A horse, cow, and some poultry went with the place. In fact, almost everything required to make it a nearly self-supporting home for a large family was ready at hand. It would furnish a quiet retreat where Grandma could write her books in some seclusion when her public labors did not press too hard.

Grandma bought the place and appointed Mrs. William Ings, who had returned with us from Europe, its caretaker. Mrs. Ings was now a widow; and with the help of a sturdy teen-ager who was working his way through college, she took on herself the responsibility of supervising the establishment. Father brought Mother and me and Auntie McComber from Burrough Valley, and Mabel came from wherever she had been sent. Father also engaged cousin Rheba Kelsey to care for us little girls. With Grandma and her helpers, and all the rest of us in residence, the house was pretty well filled. However, this situation did not last long. With her condition ever worsening, Mother was taken by carriage over the hills to the St. Helena Sanitarium, where she could receive good medical care. Mrs. McComber, of course, accompanied her.

It was at Healdsburg that I attended my first day school. I was older than the average beginner, for our family travels had interfered with my formal education. The only book learning I had thus far acquired was a little jingle:

''A-B-C-D-E-F-G, little Robin Redbreast sitting in a
    tree;
H-I-J-K-L-M-N, he made love to little Jennie Wren;
O-P-Q-R-S-T-U, I should like to marry you;
V-W-X-Y and Z [pronounced ZED in Britain], poor little Jennie blushed
    quite red.''

Mrs. William Grainger, wife of the college president, taught the first four grades of the church school. This was conducted in a room of the college building. As a teacher she possessed a remarkable combination of sweetness, gentleness, and firmness. She insisted on courtesy and prompt obedience and managed to teach sewing and gardening along with the many classes concerned with the "three R's." We held weekly missionary meetings, as was then customary in all Seventh-day Adventist schools. How happy I was when we first-graders had our turn gathering flowers from the college garden on Sunday morning to take to the patients in the children's ward of the town hospital! The missionary idea took us beyond the confines of our church institutions.

In summertime the orchard at Grandma's house was the scene of intense activity as we gathered, cut, and spread the fruit out to dry in the sun. Often neighbors would be called to help. During vacation time they would bring their children who were eager to earn a few pennies for Sabbath school offerings and spending money. After cutting for an hour or two, we younger ones usually wearied of the monotonous work and would receive an honorable discharge. Then we spent what time remained to us happily romping through the orchard and playing under the windmill.

Father learned from our medical doctors that the climate of Colorado was considered especially beneficial to tubercular patients. So, when he made his next Eastern trip, Mother and Auntie McComber accompanied him as far as Boulder, where they boarded with friends of the family for a while. At this time a person, Mary Mortensen, entered our lives and became very important to us.

For a long time I wondered where and when Father met Mary Mortensen, who mothered Mabel and me for four years while he and Grandma were in Australia. Recently I discovered the answer in an old letter. Aunt Sara McEnterfer had taken Mother's mother, Grandma Kelsey, by horse and buggy to Lake Goguac, three miles out of Battle Creek, in search of a certain young woman who was cooking for patients at the Sanitarium's lakeside summer resort. Mary Mortensen had the reputation of being an expert cook, a good seamstress, and excellent with children. She readily consented to come to Colorado to help us as soon as she could secure a release from her present position. Father rented a house at the foot of the Rocky Mountains near the future site of the Boulder Sanitarium, and there, with Grandma Kelsey and two of our friends, he established a home and sent to Healdsburg for Mabel and me.

How happy we were to be near our dear mother again! Although she was much thinner and weaker than when we had parted several months earlier, there was still the old ring of courage and cheer in her voice. As we rode out together in the carriage or sat on the front lawn in the sunshine, she would often talk to us little girls of the time when Jesus would come to take us to the beautiful mansion home the angels were helping Him prepare for us in heaven. We might be separated for a time; she was going to take a long sleep, but Jesus would wake her up, and then we could be together; and she would never, never be sick again.

When he could be with us, Father would often tell us about the missionaries who were carrying the good news of Jesus' soon coming to all parts of the world, including the faraway countries across the seas.

He would soon come to get His friends and take them to the beautiful homes He was preparing for them.

One day in Sabbath school we were told that a boat was needed to carry missionaries to the many islands in the Pacific Ocean. All the Sabbath school children were invited to earn money to pay for building the boat. When I came home I told mother about it, and she said she would help me make pen wipers and potholders that Mabel and I could sell and so earn money for our ship.

This project kept us very busy for a while. Mother helped us, of course, and did most of the hard part. Then we went around to the neighbors, selling the things we had made. We also sold popcorn balls and cookies. Mother bought us a small account book and helped us record our sales. At the end of each week we would stack our nickels and dimes and, under Mother's direction, I would make the proper entry in the account book. This task was as profitable as any lesson in arithmetic or writing. How delighted we were each Sabbath morning when we could place our earnings in the collection plate. Finally the *Pitcairn* was built. Then, to our joyful delight, "our" ship carried missionaries to the South Sea Islands.

Since there was no Adventist school in Boulder at the time, I finished my first grade in a public school. The schoolhouse stood on a hill, about a six-minute walk from the house where we were living. From our front window, Mother could watch and wave to me all the way until I entered the school building.

One day I had an exciting experience. The children in our first-grade room were lined up and marched double-file through the streets to a shop in town. There we were permitted, one by one, to hold a tube to our ear and listen to voices that seemed to come from a little box, which we called "the talking box." The voices were those of some other first-graders "way over on the other side of the city," and they answered us when we talked to them! Our excitement called forth shrieks of delight. What a story I had to tell Mamma and Mary that day! I told Grandma Kelsey and anybody else who would listen about it. I even tried to explain it to Mabel.

During Mother's long illness, Grandma White wrote many comforting letters to our father, who bore a heavy heart because the interests of

God's work required a separation from his precious Mary at a time when she needed his companionship. But whenever he suggested staying home to be with her, Mother would say without a trace of repining in her voice, "No, Will, you know I wouldn't want you to neglect God's work in order that we might be together, not while souls are at stake and your help is needed." Then I would sometimes hear them talking together of the reunion beyond the grave.

Grandma White also wrote Mother many letters full of love and tenderness and bright with the hope of an eternity spent with lovely King Jesus, whom she had served so faithfully. Often I could see Father weeping as he and Grandma Kelsey talked together.

One evening Father called Mabel and me to come to him. Very gently he told us that Mamma had fallen into the long sleep that she had told us about. He took our hands and led us into the front room, where Mother lay in a pure-white casket. In a trembling voice he read to us the words printed in golden letters on the side of the coffin: "Blessed are the dead that die in the Lord." "Blessed—happy, eternally happy," said Father, "because when Jesus comes He will wake her up. Then if we are faithful we shall all be together again." He paused for a moment and then continued, "See, her hands are now at rest. For her, there are no more heartaches, no more weariness or disappointments. When she wakes, it will be in response to the voice that calls the righteous of all ages from the tomb."

In writing to friends of her death, Father said that Mother had suffered considerably during the last three weeks, but that she had fallen asleep with a clear assurance of God's blessing and a bright hope for the future life. He explained that she had been brought to Battle Creek and buried in Oak Hill cemetery amid flowers and evergreens.

And now our father had to take up his duties with a sense of loneliness, brightened with the thought that the time of separation would be brief. He knew that when Jesus comes to take His faithful ones home there would be no more sickness, no more weeping, no more sin or sorrow."

Companionship and Separation

In Battle Creek, Father bought a home on North Kendall Street near the edge of town. It was a plain house with a lawn in front and a grape arbor and large garden space at the back. After he had the yard fenced and the house repaired and put into good living condition, we moved in. Aunt Mary Mortensen, who had so lovingly and efficiently cared for our mother during the last months of her illness, had consented to keep house for us. We were glad, for we loved Mary, and we knew she loved us. We were happy when Father told us that in the future he hoped to be at home with us much more than in the past. He had been appointed secretary of the Foreign Mission Board and to a number of important committees, and this work would keep him in Battle Creek much of the time.

Cousin May Walling, Grandma White's niece, who worked at the Review and Herald office, came to live with us. She occupied a large, front room and we also furnished one of the upstairs rooms and rented it to a lady who gave me a music lesson once a week in payment for her rent. Father bought a four-octave melodeon (organ) on which I could practice.

At this time Mabel was 4 years old, and I was nearly 9. At last it seemed that we were going to have the opportunity of becoming acquainted with our father. On weekdays we seldom saw him except at mealtimes, for he did not confine his work to regular working hours. But we eagerly looked forward to Sabbaths when we could have him all to ourselves for the entire afternoon.

As soon as the Sabbath dinner table was cleared and the dishes stacked to await their washing after sundown, we would gather up blankets and pillows, pencils, paper, and crayons, never forgetting our pocket magnifying glass. Thus equipped, we would head for the woods whenever the day was sunny. Near our house was a grove of oak trees, and here we would spread our blankets and settle down for the afternoon to enjoy the surrounding beauty and the music furnished by songbirds overhead.

Our pocket magnifier had three lenses with varying magnifications. In awe we would watch as it transformed fragments of moss into verdant forests or the petals of a wild rose into robes of richest velvet. Often we were reminded of Jesus' words inviting us to think about the flowers, which, though they take no anxious thought for what they wear, are clothed more gorgeously than King Solomon.

Then we would gather leaves and, placing them one by one under our magnifying glass, would trace the course of life-giving sap up the stem, through the channel of the midrib, and out into hundreds of tiny veins to every part of the leaf. Our minds were filled with wonder, admiration, and love for the great Creator, who had made all these fascinating things for our pleasure. This colorless, odorless fluid appeared much the same in all the leaves and flowers. Yet it supplied the life-giving substance that manifested itself in a marvelous variety of form, color, and perfume. In the giant oak, this sap built stiff, green leaves and hard-shelled acorns, while to the delicate violet growing at the foot of the tree, similar-appearing sap gave rich purple color and delicate fragrance.

How like the life of God, Father would point out, which nourishes our hearts and keeps us growing day by day into the likeness of Jesus! Although we differ from one another in appearance and characteristics, yet we can all reveal the power and love and wisdom of our Creator. Father would read to us Jesus' words about flowers and birds that never worry but accept His free gifts of sunshine and rain and fresh air, and trust Him to make them what He wants them to be.

On these little outings, Father usually brought with him one of the series of missionary biography books published by the Pacific Press. No made-up stories we ever read seemed half as thrilling as those true-life experiences of Livingstone, Carey, Judson, Moffat, Paton, and other brave people who risked their lives to bring the knowledge of God's love to those who did not know Him.

Before beginning to read, Father would always ask us to tell him the story he had read the previous Sabbath. If we could not do this satisfactorily, he would read those pages again before proceeding with a new chapter. In this way, we entered into the experiences of those brave heroes of God. In our imagination, guided by suggestions from Father, we fought lions, built huts, and calmed troubled souls and told them about a God who loved them. We ourselves were, for the moment, the missionaries of whom we were reading. And as we sat there—in Africa or India or wherever the story placed us—and told our favorite Bible stories to imaginary audiences the illusion often became very real indeed.

After we had played missionary for a time, we would gather flowers or find different kinds of leaves, then perhaps outline them and color the outlines while Father rested. The program varied from Sabbath to Sabbath. Father might take us for a long walk through the woods, returning by way of the Sanitarium, where we could leave the wildflowers we had gathered with patients sitting in wheelchairs or resting in hammocks on the lawn.

For months Mabel and I enjoyed this Sabbath-day companionship with our father until we began to feel that he belonged to us almost as much as he belonged to the General Conference. Then, without warning, our delightful together-times came to an end. The General Conference Committee asked Grandmother and Father to go to Australia for two years and help the *missionaries* who were working there.

"But, Papa," we protested, "two years is such a long time for you to be gone. Why can't we go with you?"

"Because I shall be traveling most of the time. We couldn't have any settled home. Here in Battle Creek you have a comfortable home surrounded by friends, and Mary takes good care of you. You know there is an eight-grade school here in connection with the college. Frederick Griggs, who is to be the principal, has taken a special six-months' course of study at a normal training school. Dr. Kellogg has invited Mabel to attend his Sanitarium kindergarten. Both of these schools are within a ten-minute walk of our home here. You will have Christian teachers and a chance to learn the most important things that will help to make you good missionaries."

Tearfully we kissed Papa and Grandma and Cousin May Walling

goodbye. Cousin May went in place of Sara McEnterfer, who was sick with typhoid fever. Marian Davis, Grandma's literary assistant, also accompanied them, and a new helper, Emily Campbell, joined the group. She would be bookkeeper, housemother, copyist, and all-round helper.

We promised to write Father a letter every month, and he told us to be sure to mail it in good time to catch a steamer, which would take it from San Francisco to him in Australia. He promised to write to us often and tell us all about that part of the world. At the same time he assured us that if he ever managed to establish a home of his own, he would send for us to come and live with him.

We two little girls did not realize how much harder it was for Father to leave us than it was for us to see him go. A few years back, while looking through a collection of old letters, I found one he wrote to Mary even before his ship sailed. It was in response to letters we had written to him after the party left Battle Creek. It was dated October 25, 1891, and he wrote from Oakland, California:

"Miss Mary Mortensen, Dear Sister:

"...I cannot tell you how much good it does me to hear from my dear little girls. I did not realize how I should miss them, and how hard it would really be to go off and leave them. Every sentence they write, and that you write about them, I read over and over again, and it is such a comfort to know that they are well, and that they are with someone who loves them. . . .

"Friday I came down to San Francisco and spent an hour doing my holiday shopping. I have mailed to Mabel a little musical instrument, and a walking ostrich hitched to a cart. To Ella I have sent a little puzzle, which I hope she will enjoy. I hoped that these would get there near Mabel's birthday. I also bought for Mabel's Christmas a small set of pewter dishes, and for Ella, some magnetized floating animals which will sail around in a dish of water, after the little metal wand made for the purpose. . . . "I wish you would get photographs of both Ella and Mabel, and send me half a dozen of each."[1]

Father kept his word, and we kept ours. While on board the *Alameda*, he wrote about shipboard happenings that he knew would be of interest to us:

Nov. 15, 1891

"After dinner we were wishing that we could see a ship, or a fish, or something, when along came a nice school of porpoises. They appeared to be glad to see us, and swam alongside of the ship for five or ten minutes. Some of them were four feet long, and would weigh as much as you do. They would swim along beside us, as if in a race, and then they would jump out of the water just as far as they could jump. I tell you they were pretty fellows, and they could not have jumped nicer if they had been trained.

"There are six or eight children on board, most of them about as big as Mabel. Two little boys are playing horse most of the time. And there are two little girls that talk Spanish. They have lived some years in Mexico, and there they only heard the Spanish, so they have forgotten their English, and now their mamma talks to them only in Spanish.

"I am glad that you told me so much about your school. I want you to learn to read real good, and then you can read about the places that we are to visit. Your study of geography will show you where these countries are, and then when you hear about a place, you will know where it is and what grows there."[2]

Twelve days later, after a visit to the island of Samoa, he wrote: "Yesterday was Thanksgiving, and Grandma's birthday, too. She is 64 years old. It was real nice to see her feeling so well and cheerful, after so long and tedious a journey. . . .

"Save the stamps on this envelope, for sometime you will have a book to keep all sorts of postage stamps in."[3]

Every month before "Australian mail day," all other duties and pleasures were laid aside, and we spent most of an afternoon writing our letters. Mabel dictated what she wanted to say to Aunt Mary, who wrote it down for her. In her first letter Mabel told about Jip, Mary's canary. "His cage hangs by a cord from the ceiling of the bay window where Kitty can't reach him. He sings to us every morning while we eat breakfast. We whistle to him, and he answers with a merry chirp."

The little bird provided much happy diversion for us. Each morning after breakfast Mary would fill his bath with fresh water and set it on the floor of the cage. Jip would splash, then fly to his perch and flip his wings dry. She would then clean his cage and fill his food and drink containers. On Sundays when we were home from school she would let him fly around inside the house for a few minutes.

One day the kitchen door was left open by mistake. Jip flew out and perched on a lower branch of an apple tree. We tried in vain to coax him back into the house. Then we tried to catch him, but he kept just out of our reach and talked to us saucily when we approached him. Finally, Mary boiled and mashed an egg and put it in a dish, which we placed on the floor of his cage. He could see the treat, but could not reach it from the outside. We hung the cage in the apple tree and waited for Jip to get hungry, watching every minute to see that nothing hurt him and hoping that he wouldn't fly too far away.

Jip enjoyed his freedom. He didn't know how dangerous the big world could be for little canaries. After a while, he spied the egg and hopped in through the open door to get his supper. Our bird was safe, and we were happy.

As Mary carried the cage into the house she remarked, "Now, Ella and Mabel, you can understand why your father put a fence around our house and told you never to go outside without permission. The big world is not always a safe or happy place for little boys and girls."

In response to Mabel's story about Jip, Father wrote:

"Melbourne, Australia, January 21, 1892
  to Miss Ella White, Miss Mabel White:

"It made me very happy, a few days ago, when the big bundle of letters came, to find one from Ella and one from Mabel. As soon as the letters were given to me, I hurried home and sat down by the window and would hardly stop to answer questions till the letters from home were all read.

"I was real glad to hear from Ella all about the Thanksgiving dinner at home . . . and also about the nice exercises up at the school. . . . We had our Thanksgiving dinner on the ship, and it was just like the dinner of every other day. And when Christmas came, it seemed funny enough to have [it] right in the middle of the summer.

"I was also glad that Mabel told me about your going down to Aunt Emma's and about the birdie, and the pictures. . . . It does me lots of good to know that you were well and happy and that you have lots of good friends, and lots of good times."[4]

I wrote my own letters, because Father said he would like me to do so. It was a laborious task. Many of the words I used had to be spelled out for me, and sometimes I had to erase and write them again and again to get them just right. How excited we were when the Australian mail came in! It was like having a visit with Father, and sometimes with Grandma, too. Here is a part of one of his chatty letters:

"Misses Ella and Mabel White   July 7, 1893
67 North Kendall Street
Battle Creek, Michigan.

"My Dear Daughters:
"This is mail day, and I will write to you before I go over to the *Echo* office [publishing house] and get my head so full of other matters that I shall forget what I wish to say to you. Your letters of May 18 came to hand about a week ago. . . .

"Since I wrote to you last, Sister Tenny has sold off her household goods and rented her house, and last Monday she and Ivers and Ruth left us, taking the cars [train] to Sydney and planning to sail for San Francisco on the *Monawai*, which leaves Sydney July 10.

"When I thought of my two little girls at home and how I longed to see you, I could not help wishing that the time had come for me to go too. Well, I soon put these thoughts away, for the Lord who has sent me here has been so good to me and to you, keeping you well and providing for you so many kind friends that it is ungrateful and unbecoming to make a long face about the work He has given me to do.

"What would Mary think if you should whine and cry about doing the dishes because you wanted to go and visit your dearest friends? No. You would say, That is not the way, let us hurry and do up the work first, and then our visit will be worth twice as much. This is the way I shall try to do. Work as hard as I can, and try to do in a right manner, and with an acceptable spirit what the Lord has given me to do here, and then when He brings me home to you we shall be much happier than if we had been complaining."[5]

And so the family tie with our father was kept as intact as possible through letters that made their slow way back and forth between

Australia and Battle Creek.

But Mabel and I were not the only faithful correspondents in our house. Mary sent regular reports of our progress and behavior. At least one of them would have caused me to blush with shame had I been able to read what she wrote to my father:

"Ella is doing well in her music this summer. She is Tillie's assistant in cooking. They are doing well. When I come home they have dinner all on the table, and it is well cooked. It is good practice for them. I think I have just the nicest little family. I take lots of comfort with my girls. . . . When they can get a surprise on me, then they think they have reached the highest point.

"We all went to the Lake the other day. Had a very nice time. The children went in bathing twice. We went out with Brother Landis' people; they have six children, so you may know we had a lively time."[6]

"I let Ella take one lesson a week in music. She was so anxious to keep on with it. I fear it will be too much for her. I think I shall have her drop music after a short time. Ella does not need any pushing when it comes to mental work. She has never fallen in love with physical labor; still she is gaining on that point.

"Ella does a thing from principle, and she realizes that she can never be a perfect girl or woman till she is a good housekeeper. What she does she does well after she has had a few lessons in it.

"If I should allow Ella she would spend a good share of her time in building air castles and laying great schemes for making money. While I think a little of that is all right for a child, too much, I think, is injurious to their best development.

"Mabel is just the opposite. She loves to work and is just as happy as a lark when she is helping me. Mabel has no special taste for study, is very quick to learn when she sets about it. She never worries over anything. When she has her mind on her Sabbath school lessons she can tell the whole story by my reading them over once or at the most twice.

"I do not want you to get the impression that Ella is not willing to help me, for she is. There is nothing that delights them any better than when they can do some of my work when I am away, and surprise me."[7]

References
[1] W. C. White letter to Mary Mortensen, Oct. 25, 1891.
[2] W. C. White letter to Ella White, Nov. 15, 1891.
[3] W. C. White letter to Ella White, Nov. 27, 1891.
[4] W. C. White letter to Ella and Mabel White, Jan. 21, 1892.
[5] W. C. White letter to Ella and Mabel White, July 7, 1893.
[6] Mary Mortensen letter to W. C. White, Aug. 13, 1894.
[7] Mary Mortensen letter to W. C. White, Nov. 7, 1894.

Childhood Days in Battle Creek

The Australian mail came each month, bringing the promised letters from Papa. In them he described Australia's lovely parks and gardens, adorned with tropical and semitropical trees and shrubbery and gorgeous with bright-colored flowers and elegantly plumaged birds. The houses and towns were not very different from those in American cities. He had not seen as many aborigines as he had expected. These people, who had come to Australia long before the Europeans, now made up a much smaller portion of the population than did the native Indians of the United States.

Papa told us about individuals and families of Sabbathkeepers who had never seen a Seventh-day Adventist minister or Bible instructor but who had learned of present truth from papers sent them from the United States. Often he found the people lonely and discouraged. They were glad to learn that soon ministers and teachers would arrive to instruct them further in Bible truth. Father encouraged them to look forward to the time when they would have their own church building in which to hold services. Eventually, he hoped, there would be a sanitarium and a college, where their sick could be cared for and their young people educated as gospel workers.

Evangelists and Bible teachers were needed to bring the good news of Jesus' soon coming to the people of Australia and New Zealand, and to teach the people living on the thousands of islands scattered over the vast Pacific Ocean about the true and living God who loves them. There were workers' homes to be built and churches to be erected. Tents in which to hold evangelistic meetings were needed. Many books and papers had to be published. So many things needed doing, but "we have so little money with which to accomplish all this," he wrote.

One day we received a letter from Grandma telling us that Papa was traveling third class on the steamers in order to save money to help students attend the Bible school. When we read that letter, Mary and Mabel and I held a serious conference. We knew that Father received a very small wage, as did all Adventist ministers in those early days when there was little money in the conference treasury. We decided that we would spend as little as possible and that we would make every penny count so he would not need to send us so much. In this way he would have more with which to help the work in Australia.

The next question was what we children could do to help. Charlie Colcord, who lived across the street from us, carried the supply of milk for his family in a tin pail from a farmhouse about a mile away. We were buying our milk from a man who delivered it by pony cart from door to door. When we heard his whistle I would hurry out with a pan and he would dip our two quarts out of a ten-gallon can. He charged five cents a quart for the milk. The farmer folk sold it at their door for four cents. I decided to carry our milk as Charlie did and thus save about fifty cents a month.

"What can I do?" Mabel asked.

"You can wash the breakfast dishes," said Mary, "so Ella will have time to go for the milk before school." Mabel didn't like washing dishes, but the thought of helping Papa made the task more pleasant.

As the days went by we found many ways in which to save nickels and dimes. We decided that when we went to Lake Goguac for a swim we would walk one way, thus saving three five-cent streetcar fares. Mary said that walking would make us strong, and besides, she thought the water felt extra good after the three-mile walk on a warm summer day. We always rode home.

Sometimes we could spare extra strawberries or vegetables from our garden. Asparagus was the most popular, and a patch growing alongside the fence furnished many a bunch. I sold asparagus for five cents a bunch, taking orders on my way home after school and making deliveries on my way to school in the morning. We kept a record of our sales and faithfully paid our tithe at the end of each month. No money was spent for toys or candy. We had a wagon, but aside from that we made our own toys.

In the summertime an ice-cream wagon visited our street every day. Once a year, on the Fourth of July, we indulged, sitting out in the shade of the apple tree and making our yearly treat last as long as possible. On Christmas morning we were permitted to invite our playmates to share a candy-pull in our kitchen.

Next door to us lived a dear old lady known as Grandma Hunt. She had a pony and buggy, and sometimes when she went on errands she would take Mabel and me for a ride. One day she took us to the lake for a picnic lunch and swim. About three o'clock in the afternoon she called to us, "Come, girls; it's time to get out of the water and get ready to go home."

But we thought otherwise. No more was said, and we accepted silence as consent. It was about five o'clock when we started our homeward jaunt. On the way Grandma Hunt startled us with the calm but emphatic statement, "Ella and Mabel, this is the last time I shall take you swimming, because you did not obey me when I told you it was time to get out of the water."

She kept her word. Sometimes she would take us other places, but never again to the lake. Many a day as we watched her drive out of her yard we would ask each other, "Do you suppose she is going to Lake Goguac?" We were always left to wonder. Punishments in those days, as I remember, were prompt, appropriate, and effective, and always of a nature to cause us to regret our misdeeds.

The summer after Father and Grandmother went to Australia, Aunt Mary took us girls with her on a visit to her home in Minnesota. We spent most of the summer playing and working with her younger brothers and sisters on the family's 160-acre farm. We raked hay, and shocked wheat, picked berries, and chased grasshoppers. What I enjoyed most was jumping from the barn loft onto a pile of hay. We came home sun-tanned and happy and ready to settle down to another year of school.

That winter I attended the eight-grade church school conducted in the college building. Mabel was enrolled in the Sanitarium kindergarten and Mary attended classes in nursing.

After school hours and during summer vacation days our street, being free from traffic, became a favorite playground for the neighborhood boys and girls, and sometimes we were permitted to join the sport.

One day early in July I saw Charlie Colcord and some other boys playing with firecrackers on the sidewalk in front of our house. Each boy would place a giant firecracker inside a tin can, light it, then scurry a safe distance away and watch to see how far the can would be tossed. I begged Charlie to give me just one firecracker, so I might join the game, but I was promptly told that "this game is too dangerous for little girls," which did not please me at all.

I must have told somebody that I wanted some giant firecrackers, because my music teacher, who lived in the room upstairs, gave me five cents to invest in them. With that much money I could buy six giant crackers and join the fun. I laid the nickel careful away in the top drawer of my dresser.

About this time the Southern Missionary Society was in need of funds with which to carry on gospel evangelism in the Southern States. They had sent little collection boxes to the Adventist churches in and around Battle Creek. In the lid of each box was a slot for dropping in nickels, dimes, and quarters. On one side of the box were printed the words "Self-denial Box," and on the other side "Freely ye have received, freely give."

We set our box on a ledge by the kitchen door, where we had to pass it every time we went in or out of the house. As I passed by, it seemed to say, "Ella, you have a nickel upstairs. Are you going to spend it selfishly or are you going to give it to the Lord to help teach some soul the way of salvation?"

Every time I passed that little box it seemed to repeat the question—"What are you going to do with that nickel?" A battle was on. It was one of the fiercest battles with self that I ever fought, and it raged nearly three days. "What about that nickel, Ella?"

"I'll give it to Jesus. Oh, but I do want to play the firecracker game!"

At last I could endure it no longer. I ran upstairs, picked up the nickel, and dropped it into the box. I was so happy then that I wondered how I ever could have thought of exploding money in firecrackers just to have a little fun when the work of Jesus needed it so much. I never regretted my decision.

A little later that morning Aunt Mary sent me to the grocery store around the corner to order a fifty-pound sack of flour. The delivery boy was busy on his rounds, but Mary needed the flour at once to finish the baking, so I hauled it home in our wagon. As I was about to leave, the grocery lady said, "Wait a minute, Ella."

She disappeared into the store and a minute later came out with a Roman candle in her hand, saying as she gave it to me, "This is your reward for acting as my delivery boy."

The news of the Roman candle quickly spread throughout the neighborhood. That evening at sunset, a group of children gathered in our yard to see it fired off. Charlie was there, of course.

"Oh, Ella, let me hold it. I can send it much higher than you can."

Giving him a disdainful look I announced, "This game is too dangerous for little boys." Then sister and I each had a few seconds of delight holding the candle, while all the other children stood around watching the bright multicolored balls and stars and spark clusters light the sky with glory.

In the basement of the college building was a large gymnasium where we students practiced marches and gymnastics under the direction of Dr. William George, who somehow found time between his duties at the Sanitarium to come to the college and direct the students in calisthenics and exercises with dumbbells, clubs, and wands. He drilled us also in correct positions for sitting, standing and walking.

The great school treats of the year were the magic-lantern shows. Once a month we were permitted to climb the long flights of stairs—"in perfect order and decorum"—to a large room under the belfry, where we were shown marvelous things by means of a spluttering, popping lantern. The more it spluttered and popped, the more fun it was for us!

Sometimes the lantern went completely out, to the delight of certain boys, who enjoyed throwing spitballs and playing tricks more than viewing the wonders of travel or the mysteries of science. Rumor has it that in later years some of those naughty boys became very successful teachers and disciplinarians.

The nearest approach to the teaching of industries in the Battle Creek church school at that time was the introduction of sloyd, a sort of artistic carpentry by which we were taught to make fancy objects such as handkerchief boxes, bookends, picture frames, place mats, penholders, and all sorts of pretty things for Christmas gifts.

In order to encourage the community in a late-dinner, no-supper regimen, our midday recess was scheduled at one o'clock instead of at the usual noon hour. The two-meal-a-day program ceased to be considered a life-and-death matter after our reformers led the members away from the custom of loading dinner tables with a large variety of incompatible and indigestible foods such as rich cakes, pastries, and desserts. Jams and preserves, which often stood on the back of the kitchen stove for hours "cooking down," were declared by well-informed physicians to require six or seven hours for digestion. Our health instructors often repeated to us the injunction that the tired, overworked stomach was as much in need of rest as its owner.

We had been instructed not to discard flesh foods entirely until suitable substitutes could be found. In harmony with that instruction, we occasionally stewed a savory joint in the soup pot and once in a while indulged in potato-and-meat hash for breakfast. But one day Mary brought home from her cooking class a report from a young man who worked in a butcher shop. The report was of such a nature that it led her to decide never again to serve flesh food on our table.

Four-year-old Mabel was particularly fond of hash. She pleaded, "Aunt Mary, why can't we have any more hash?"

Seeking for an answer that would appeal to the child's tender heart, Mary replied, "Suppose you had a pet lamb, Mabel, and some men killed it and cooked it, just so they could have hash to eat. Would you like that?"

For a moment Mabel looked puzzled. Then she came up with a brilliant suggestion.

"You know those cats that fight and squeal under the bay window? Nobody'd care if we made hash out of them."

Aunt Mary smiled. We decided to continue relying on milk, eggs, and well-cooked legumes for our necessary proteins, even though we had to spend weary hours "picking over" dry beans and peas to free them from tiny gravel stones and litter before they could be transformed into nourishing and appetizing dishes.

During the winter months there were few, if any, fresh fruits or salad vegetables on the market. Frozen foods were a commodity of the future, and canned vegetables were only beginning to make their appearance in stores. From November till June, potatoes and onions, cabbage and beans, rice and cereals, were our staple articles of food. Bananas were an expensive luxury. And oranges? Well, we could be quite sure of finding *one* in our Christmas stocking.

Still, there were always pumpkins and apples and home-canned fruits in the cellar. These, with Mary's delicious home-baked, whole-wheat bread and fresh dairy milk (which was always boiled before being used), enabled our family to survive and keep well, although the meals were at times somewhat monotonous.

Then, joy of joys, *peanut butter* made its appearance! Here is how it happened: One of the kitchen helpers at the Sanitarium overbaked a batch of peanuts and was told that he must pay for them.

"All right," he said, "if I pay for the peanuts they belong to me."

Taking them home, he shelled, winnowed, and ground them up, and added a little salt. The next morning he took some of the sticky but flavorful paste to Dr. Kellogg, who willingly sampled it.

"That tastes good," remarked the doctor. "What will you take for the rights on this new food product?"

"Twenty-five dollars!" cheerfully replied the young man, naming what seemed to him an astronomical sum.

"Sold!" exclaimed Dr. Kellogg. Thus a new protein food was soon on the market. The Health Food Company failed to patent this product, and soon peanut growers, as well as manufacturers of hand-operated peanut butter mills, were doing a thriving business. Nut butter of various sorts supplied the foundation ingredient for many meat substitutes and the "protein problem" for vegetarians evaporated or was reduced to a minimum.

After a time Mary found a way to supplement the family income. As she became acquainted with patients at the Sanitarium, she arranged to give day care to their small children. In order to do this, she dropped her studies for a time, and our house took on the aspect of a small nursery. But, desiring to resume her nursing and homemaking classes, she closed the day-care center after a few months and took in several older youth who were in need of mothering while attending school. The young people, of course, added activity and interest to our home.

Dr. Kellogg had built a commodious house in the oak grove near our

Kendall Street home and transferred his large family of orphan children to it, along with the kindergarten and classes for mothers. This was a convenient arrangement for Mary. At school time in the morning our house was closed, and all of us children trudged off with lunch pails. Mary took Mabel with her and left her at the kindergarten where she mingled with the other children.

Our good neighbor, Grandma Hunt, moved away and a new family, the Landises, occupied the house next door. The children were Esther, Wilma, Charlie, Mayte, and Lloyd; and soon after they moved in, Freddie was born. What rousing games we had together! With the coming of the Landis tribe, life took on a new luster for Mabel and me. We applied ourselves most diligently to the fun at hand.

Eagerly we looked forward to the first heavy snow, when we could build snowmen, snow houses, and snow forts, and engage in snow battles. For the snow houses we would roll four huge balls and place them close together, fill in the chinks with more snow, packing the walls firmly, then hollow out a room inside. After that we would build our "snow family" and stand them around the house.

When winter was passed, May Day brought its fun and frolic. As soon as school was out on the afternoon of April 30, we would be searching field and meadow for the first wildflowers or robbing our window gardens and slowly awakening pansy beds. Then, each carrying a bright-colored paper basket, we would sally forth under the cover of dusk, hang our basket on a doorknob, knock, and run. Catching the donor was part of the game, but failing this, you were at least supposed to guess who had hung the basket on your door.

Golden days that now seem so long ago!

We Went to Church

Mabel and I attended Sabbath school and church services with Aunt Mary in the big "Dime Tabernacle" a building so named because the cast of its construction had been met by individual contributions of a dime each month from the members of the church (or at least that was the plan). It was a beautiful, commodious building, capable of comfortably seating more than three thousand persons. On special occasions, such as General Conference sessions, it often held four thousand or more, with people standing in the aisles and sitting on the gallery steps.

The Sabbath school was conducted then much as it is now, with senior, youth, intermediate, primary, and kindergarten divisions, but no cradle roll or nursery. The senior division met in the main auditorium, the young people in the balcony, and the children's groups in three large wings of the church, which were separated from one another and from the main auditorium by partitions that could be rolled back, making one large room of the entire lower floor. Mabel was in the kindergarten, and I in the primary. Mary taught a kindergarten class.

At this time Grandma White's nephew "Uncle Frank" Belden was introducing kindergarten methods into the Sabbath schools and was using the beginners' division of the Tabernacle school as his demonstration ground. With the help of Lillian Afalter, an expert kindergarten teacher, Uncle Frank had prepared a well-illustrated teachers' guidebook that gave the lesson story in simple words, ready to be told to the little ones. It also showed how to demonstrate the story using stick figures for people, small wooden blocks for houses, tiny woolly sheep, and various objects representing hills and lakes, tents and cottages, forests and gardens.

This guidebook, *Bible Object Lessons*, contained many beautiful pictures copied from famous paintings of scenes from the life of Christ.

It also had new songs composed by Uncle Frank, which he taught us from Sabbath to Sabbath. In the primary division each teacher illustrated the lesson on a small blackboard set on a low, round table around which the class members were seated.

On Sabbath mornings the partition between the primary and kindergarten divisions was rolled back, and we often enjoyed a half-hour's "sing" together under the leadership of the composer himself. Uncle Frank taught us those songs so well that now, many years later, many of them come readily to my mind.

One morning Uncle Frank told us that he had composed the first stanza of a new song on his way to Sabbath school, and now he would teach it to us. Soon we were all singing the words:

> 'Tis love that makes us happy,
> 'Tis love that smooths the way;
> It helps us mind, it makes us kind
> To others every day.

That song has circled the world and become a favorite with children everywhere.

Another favorite song of mine was "Angels Are Building Fair Mansions Above." It could be sung in relays, the leader asking the question: "Shall we be there? Shall we be there?" Then we children would respond with the chorus:

> "We must be there, We must be there,
> Safe in the beautiful city of gold.
> We must be there, We must be there,
> When the bright gates unfold."

Teachers' meetings were conducted on Wednesday evenings an hour before prayer meeting and were well attended. For a time, a record was kept of attendance and punctuality just as in the Sabbath school itself. Teachers rehearsed the lesson in turn until they became experts in telling the story and demonstrating it with miniature objects, much as is done today.

I can remember only one of my teachers clearly. He was a college student who taught the class of little girls to which I belonged. One Sabbath afternoon he took us for a long walk into the country. At Christmas time he presented each of us with a copy of Grandma's new book, *Steps to Christ*, in which gilt-edged and gilt-lettered he had underlined his favorite passages in gold ink. I thought it very beautiful, and I read those marked passages over and over until I knew them by heart.

I also remember a certain guest speaker who gave the lesson review one Sabbath. He caused considerable merriment by drawing on the blackboard a spider with only six legs.

At the close of Sabbath school, Mary, Mabel, and I would climb the steps to our favorite seat by the balcony railing. From this vantage point we children could look down on the people below and amuse ourselves counting heads when the "firstly, secondly, thirdly, fourthly, . . . tenthly" of certain long-winded preachers became too protracted.

When Mary discovered how we were occupying our time, she inaugurated a plan that she hoped would direct our thoughts into more profitable channels. She provided Mabel with pencil and paper and asked her to make a mark every time the preacher spoke the word *God*, or *Jesus*, or the name of some Bible character who might be the subject of his discourse. I was expected to remember at least one story he told and to repeat it at the dinner table after church. I thought my assignment a difficult one, because, as I complained to Mary, "hardly any of the preachers ever tell any stories at all!"

Somtimes on Sabbath afternoons Mary would take us to attend the callboys' meeting at the Sanitarium church. I was awed as I listened to Dr. David Paulson tell of his boyhood struggles with tormenting fears because of his lost, sinful condition, and of the great joy he experienced when he learned to trust Jesus. Usually there would be a testimony meeting in which the callboys themselves would stand up and speak of the victories they had gained over temptations and evil habits, and of their desire to witness for Jesus before the patients.

Mary's youngest sister, Tillie, came to live with us so she could attend church school. I enjoyed going with her to student meetings in the college chapel. I remember one testimony meeting that lasted until nearly midnight. The leader could not close it, because so many of the students wanted to testify, praising God for blessings they had received at the school. Our Christian teachers were much in earnest, and many godless youths who came to the college were converted before the school term closed and later became gospel workers.

In the Tabernacle church there were also stirring revivals, during which time the Holy Spirit's presence was especially manifest. At one Week of Prayer meeting, members of the congregation came forward voluntarily and took off such jewelry as bracelets, necklaces, and gold watch chains and laid them on the platform at the feet of the ministers, saying as they did so that they wished to have these needless ornaments sold and the money put into the Lord's treasury.

Occasionally we went to hear Dr. Kellogg's lectures to his patients in the Sanitarium parlor. At the close of his talk, if we didn't get away before he caught sight of us, he would call us into his office, where busy man though he was, he took time to talk with us. We would share with him the latest news from Australia, for he and Papa were great friends. He would inquire about our health and ask whether we needed anything. Whatever our wants might be—an inhaler, a bottle of nasal spray, or a jar of medicated ointment—he would have his office nurse wrap up and give to us. Then he would send us on our way after advising us to spend much time in the sunshine and to exercise in the open air.

The Sanitarium was an interesting place to visit on weekday evenings. The nursing students frequently put on demonstrations, showing how to administer fomentations, salt glows, sweating packs, sitz baths, and other hot- and cold-water treatments.

During the spring of 1894 two young women, Georgia Burrus, a house-to-house Bible instructor in the California Conference, and Myrtle Griffis, from the Oakland City Mission, were appointed to go to India and begin pioneer work among the women. While arrangements were being made for their departure, Myrtle stayed at our home and visited with her friend Mary Mortensen.

It soon appeared that Myrtle was not well. As she rapidly grew worse, all thought of her going to India was abandoned, and the Sanitarium physicians expressed the fear that she had only a short time to live. But Myrtle felt strongly impressed that the Lord had work for her to do and that He would heal her. She requested that special prayer be offered, and it was arranged for three of the leading Battle Creek ministers to come to our house and have a prayer and anointing season. The appointment was set for Sunday forenoon.

On Friday evening, at the commencement of the Sabbath, our little family gathered as usual around the heater in the front room. As we studied our Sabbath school lesson the presence of holy angels seemed very real to us, and we spoke of it to one another. Myrtle was lying on the couch breathing heavily and suffering great pain.

"Children," said Mary gently, "let us pray for Myrtle. God loves to answer the prayers of children." So we all knelt and had a short season of prayer, in which each took part. To us it seemed almost as if we could reach out and touch the healing robe.

When we rose from our knees Myrtle was sitting up, her blanket thrown back. There was not a tremor of weakness in her voice as she said, "Children, the Lord has heard your prayers and answered them. He has healed me! I feel a new surge of life in my body. All the pain is gone!"

When the ministers arrived Sunday morning, Myrtle said to them:

"I have no objection to your praying for me, but healing has already been accomplished. God has answered the children's prayers." After that, Myrtle rapidly regained her strength. Though entirely free from the disease that had threatened her life, she was advised by her physicians against going to India, and Georgia courageously proceeded alone.

Myrtle said, "I think the Lord must have other plans for me," and so He had. Not long after this she married Calvin Parker, an oldtime sweetheart, and together they devoted their lives to gospel work in Fiji and other Pacific islands and also in Australia. In the New Hebrides they bravely faced savage cannibals. On his initial visit to one of the islands, Calvin was made to sit down on a rock while the village cook felt him over to see whether he would make a good pot roast. Just at that tense moment, a man with a badly ulcerated sore on his leg appeared. Calvin seized his medicine case and went to work. The Lord blessed the treatment applied, and the natives agreed that they would wait and give this new medicine man time to treat all their ailments before they stewed him!

Before the end of that school year, a great revival occurred in Battle Creek. Beginning with the students at college level, it reached all the way down to the primary grades. Elder McCoy came into our schoolroom and talked to us children, explaining what it meant to be a true Christian. Very quickly each roomful of children became a baptismal class.

One Sabbath afternoon, in the Tabernacle, there was a baptism of more than one hundred candidates, and I was one of them. Two ministers officiated, and we entered the baptistry in groups of four or five. As my companions and I came up out of the water, the congregation was singing, "I will follow Thee, my Saviour, whereso'er my lot may be."

Never have I regretted taking that step early in life. The companionship of my Saviour has been sweet, although at times not as close as I might desire. He has become more and more precious to me through the years.

A New Prophet?

One Sabbath morning Elder Alonzo T. Jones preached a startling sermon from the pulpit of the Tabernacle church. We all gave him our full attention.

A new prophet! A new prophet among us? That is what he was saying. Her name was Anna Phillips. She had been given several visions, Elder Jones told us, and some of her friends had been copying them and sending them out to the people. Those who received the material said that they sounded very much like the visions of Ellen G. White. Elder Jones had some of Anna Phillips' writings with him at the desk and was reading from them. He also had some of Mrs. White's testimonies. They lay side by side.

After asking how we could know whether or not the messages were from heaven he spoke of the Shepherd and His sheep. "The true sheep follow the Shepherd because they know His voice," he stated.

He read from Mrs. White's testimonies, then asked, "Do you hear the voice?" Answering himself, he said, "Yes, we hear the voice." Next he read from the visions of Anna Phillips and repeated the question and the answer, "Do you hear the voice? Yes, we hear the voice; it is the same voice."

Elder Jones reasoned that because Anna Phillips' visions sounded so much like the testimonies of Ellen White, they must be from the same source. By their similarity we could know that her visions were also the voice of God speaking to us, but through a different messenger.

When the meeting closed, the building did not empty as quickly as usual. No one seemed inclined to hurry home to dinner. People stood talking in the aisles and vestry, and on the sidewalks and lawns little groups conversed earnestly.

"Do you think Elder Jones is right?" some asked. "We have confidence in him; yet he might be wrong. This just might be one of the devil's counterfeits. We wonder what Sister White would say about this?" Others said, "Let us pray that God will send light."

None of the folks in our house had ever heard of Anna Phillips, but she was known to some of the church leaders as a godly, devoted young woman and an earnest Christian. Yet these leaders felt that the church should wait for stronger evidence before accepting her as a prophet.

In the Tabernacle congregation that Sabbath morning sat a college student by the name of W. M. Adams. He has left an interesting firsthand account of the remarkable manner in which the prayers for light were answered the very next day. He wrote:

"On Sunday morning I went to the Review and Herald office and purchased a postal card. I had just stepped to the writing board when Elder Jones came in.

"'Any mail?' he inquired in his characteristic way. I watched, and saw a long envelope bearing the return address of Mrs. E. G. White. I was immediately interested, for I recalled his sermon the day before concerning Anna Phillips. I stood and closely watched him as he sat down on a bench and began to read. I saw that he was deeply affected, for tears began to flow freely. He read on.

"Presently, Elder A. O. Tait came in, and Elder Jones said, "'Oscar, come here. Sit down. You heard me preach that sermon yesterday?'

"'Yes,' replied Elder Tait.

"'Well, read this,' he said, as he handed him the testimony he had just received from Sister White.

"Here is a part of what Elder Tait read. . . .

'Elder A. T. Jones

'Dear Brother:

'I have a message for you. Did you suppose that God has commissioned you to take the burden of presenting the visions of Anna Phillips, reading them in public, and uniting them with the testimonies the Lord has been pleased to give me? No, the Lord has not laid upon you this burden. He has not given you this work to do.
. . .

'How is it, my brother, that you have taken up these communications, and presented them before the people, weaving them in with the testimonies God has given Sister White? Where is your evidence that these are of God? You cannot be too careful how you hear, how you receive, how you believe.'

" 'Who told Sister White a month ago,' said Elder Jones, 'that I was going to preach that sermon about Anna Phillips as a prophetess?'

" 'Ah, you know, Alonzo, you know,' declared Elder Tait, in his calm, yet firm way.

" 'Yes, I do know. God knew what I would do, and He impressed Sister White a month before I preached the sermon to send the testimony that I am wrong. Look at that date, "March 15, 1894." I am wrong.'

"The next Sabbath Elder Jones read part of the testimony sent him fully thirty days prior to the date he preached his sermon, mailed from Melbourne, Australia. It reproved him for his position taken concerning Anna Phillips' testimonies. He said, 'I am wrong, and I confess it. Now I am right.' That ended the matter."

This incident was later published in the columns of the *Review and Herald* of July 7, 1949.

Anna Phillips did not intentionally seek to deceive the church. She was sincere in sending out her visions. In them was the manifestation of supernatural power. But she did not recognize their source. God saved her and also all the church from deception by sending them the warning message to keep them from being deceived in the days to follow.

In another letter written about that time, Grandma expressed sorrow that the writings of Anna Phillips had been grasped and scattered broadcast "with so little test and proving." She further wrote: "Woven in them will be statements that will lead to extremes, and to wrong actions on the part of those who accept them. . . . Movements will be made that bear not the divine credentials, doubts will be cast upon the true work of the Spirit of prophecy. And the testimonies that God sends to the people will bear the stigma of these false utterances."

Grandma also sounded a warning for all future time. "There will be those who claim to have visions. When God gives you clear evidence that the vision is from Him, you may accept it, but do not accept it on any other evidence; for people are going to be led more and more astray in foreign countries and in America."

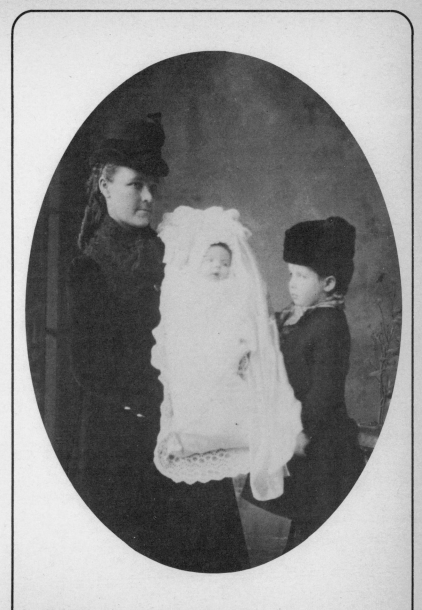

A rare photograph of Mary Kelsey White with her daughters, Mabel and Ella.

This 1888 photo shows 6-year-old Ella and Mabel. The little girls would still have their mother for two years.

Ella and Mabel, resplendent in matching dresses, pose with a sober group of young ladies in Australia. Their stepmother, May Lacey White, began immediately to improve the appearance of the little girls, who had been orphans for a number of years.

Elder W. C. White and May Lacey White hold their twin sons, Henry and Herbert, born in 1896. Mabel and Ella are standing.

This picture of Dores and Ella Robinson was probably taken around the time of their wedding in 1905.

Dores and Ella Robinson posed with their children, Virgil and Mabel, and relatives in 1911. Dores' sister, Gladys, is standing behind Ella.

Ella and Dores in 1924 with their growing family, which now includes Gladys.

In 1913 Ellen White posed for this photograph with her family. W. C. and May White are at the right of the picture. Ella and her husband, Dores Robinson, are at the left. Mabel White Workman and her husband, Wilfred, are standing with the twins, Henry and Herbert White. Little Virgil and Mabel Robinson sit in front of their parents. Arthur and Grace White complete the picture. W. C. and May's youngest child, Francis, is not shown.

Ella Robinson poses with her children Virgil and Mabel about 1914. The horse and buggy were the same that she used for her colporteuring and aluminum-ware selling.

Ella White Robinson with her father, W. C. White, and her son, Virgil, in 1936.

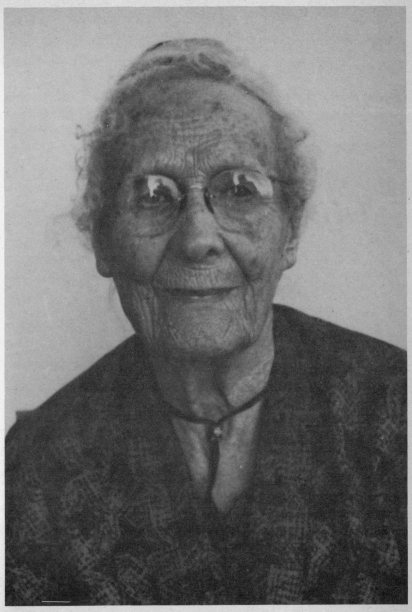

May Lacey White Currow. After the death of W. C. White in 1937, May married Arthur Currow.

Ella Robinson about the time Over My Shoulder *was written.*

Ella Robinson, a spry 94, at her typewriter.

Anna Phillips accepted the correction given her through God's established messenger and humbly confessed that she had been in error. She took up her former labors in the church, and continued working as a sincere and successful Bible instructor until shortly before her death. She died a loyal Seventh-day Adventist.

General Conference sessions were always exciting times for those living in Battle Creek. On Sabbaths the great Tabernacle would be filled to capacity. Delegates were present from nearly all parts of the United States and from several European countries and Australia. The four hundred Battle Creek College students were usually there in a body, and the nurses and helpers from the Sanitarium would also attend as many meetings as their duties permitted. Though the congregation might be uncomfortably crowded at times, no one became tired or "counted heads" while missionaries told of the way in which the Advent message was advancing in many parts of the world.

Our good missionary ship, the *Pitcairn*, had transported Bible teachers and ministers to a number of the Pacific islands, and from these centers the good news of Jesus' soon coming was being carried to many other islands. Literature provided by the missionary societies was being sent through the mails, or tied in bundles and put on board ships bound for distant shores. Ship missionaries were busy in many ports.

Evangelistic centers and Bible training schools had been established in some of the large cities of America. Colporteurs were carrying the good word from city to city. A beginning was being made in the Southern States, also in Hawaii and the West Indies. The denomination had two publishing houses, three colleges, and two sanitariums in the United States and some treatment rooms in Europe.

Seventh-day Adventists were beginning to send missionaries to Africa and the Orient. Mission centers and companies of believers were multiplying in Sweden, Norway, Switzerland, Germany, France, England, and Denmark. National workers were being trained in these new areas. Gospel-filled tracts were being translated, published, and scattered by literature evangelists in many of the principal languages of Europe. God's work of preparing a people to meet the King of kings was steadily moving forward in many parts of the world.

Elder S. N. Haskell had been to Africa, India, China, and Japan, where he had baptized the first Seventh-day Adventist convert. There were two or three believers in Hong Kong, where Brother Abram LaRue was working alone, supporting himself by selling Adventist literature to English-speaking officers and crew on vessels that visited Hong Kong harbor. He had personally arranged and financed the translation and publication of the first piece of Adventist literature in the Chinese language. Now, with the assistance of a Christian gentleman whom he had met on his way to China, LaRue was circulating Adventist tracts and periodicals.

Elder Haskell had brought back word from his world-circling tour that there were favorable opportunities in certain heathen lands for the opening of missions, if only workers could be found. He pleaded for Christian men and women who would dedicate their lives to the fulfilling of Christ's commission to carry the gospel of salvation to every creature under heaven. Living in Battle Creek was a thrilling thing in those days, particularly while the General Conference sessions were in progress.

The conference usually continued for a little more than two weeks, after which the delegates returned to their various fields of labor and life for the rest of us resumed its quiet round of study, work, and play.

Once in a while Barnum's wild animal show would visit the town. A mammoth tent was pitched and the townspeople were caught up in exciting entertainment for two or three days. Adventists were not supposed to attend these shows, which were often accompanied by unbecoming and immodest exhibitions. But we could and did watch the parade and follow it from street to street as long as we could keep within hearing distance of the calliope.

One evening in early spring, a new kind of parade formed. It began where we heard a shout from down the street, "They're coming! They're coming!" We took our positions by the gate in front of our house just in time to see the first bicycle spin past. Then others followed, hundreds of them, two abreast. It was a beautiful sight—lights flashing, horns honking, the riders shouting back and forth as they tried to outdistance one another. As I remember, they were more than half an hour wheeling past our house.

Not long after this a letter was received from Grandma White reproving the members of the Battle Creek church for their extravagant outlay of money for bicycles. She spoke of the "bicycle craze," and of the money that was spent "to gratify an enthusiasm in this direction that might better . . . have been invested in building houses of worship where they are greatly needed."

At that time the price of a new bicycle was $150, while the wage of a laborer was only one or two dollars a day. Thousands of dollars must have been invested in bicycles for the sole purpose of participating in the parade that we had watched from our gate. In the letter, Grandma said that these things were working counter to the message God had given His people to proclaim in order to arouse the world to the great event that is just before us.

She further sounded a warning that anything that can be made to absorb means in meeting supposed wants in any direction, Satan will use with an intensity of purpose, that our people may be induced to spend their time and money.

Several conscientious employees of the Review and Herald, who had purchased bicycles for the purpose of getting back and forth to their dinner at noon, promptly sold them and carried cold lunches. As the price rapidly dropped, and with the advice of wise counselors who assured them that bicycles were not only permissible but practical when used for the accomplishment of necessary labor, these conscientious souls purchased bicycles again.

Last Days in Battle Creek

How eagerly Mabel and I looked forward to our monthly mail-chats with Papa! He was so interested in everything that interested us. He wanted to know about the kittens and the garden and the sweet peas, and the little blind boy I was reading to on Sunday mornings. He hoped the mother bird that was making her nest in the basket we hung on the back porch would complete it and that Mabel and I would be so gentle that she would always feel safe when near us. Would I send him that difficult problem in fractions that I wrote about? He would like to see whether he could work it.

Father said that he was sending us a stamp album and an envelope of foreign stamps to paste into it. He hoped we wouldn't waste any more time on the "funny language" we were inventing, because he was afraid it would ruin our pronunciation. He told us all about his third-class passage on a steamer going to New Zealand so we wouldn't worry about him any more. He said that often there were as many as thirty or forty passengers in one room; but the rooms were large and clean, and the passengers had pleasant times talking together.

Mabel and I were intrigued with the idea that things were "upside down" in Australia. Someone had told us that certain birds in that country had their feathers pointing toward their heads, and that cherries grew with the pits on the outside. Father wrote about a small tree bearing fruit that resembled a cherry, but with the meat on the inside and a hard stonelike shell on the outside. He also said that in some parts of the country there were birds that looked as if their feathers had been rubbed the wrong way.

One day Papa's monthly letter told of gifts that would soon arrive. "I sent a message to each of you by Miss Grattidge," he wrote, "and a little parcel for each. (Miss Grattidge was traveling to Battle Creek to take the nurse's course at the Sanitarium.) "The round parcel is for Ella," he wrote. The package contained the egg of a large Australian bird called the emu. It was nearly as large as an ostrich egg. On the egg was a picture, not painted, but engraved, showing two emu birds out on the plains, and a black man, a native Australian, creeping up to spear the birds. The emus were clumsy-looking fellows, but the shell of the egg was remarkable. It had three distinct layers, each of a different color. The outside layer was black. Inside this was a layer of blue, then one of pure white. The carving in these three colors was very pretty.

Mabel's parcel contained the tail of a lyre bird, a large, beautiful tail, the shape of a lyre or harp. Father explained that these birds were funny fellows. The male bird would get up on a little mound of sand and go through all kinds of antics to show off his beautiful feathers, while his mate admired him. The bird was not proud of his plain head, so he hid it under his wing and then peeked through his wing to see if he was receiving his due amount of admiration.

The new curios were placed on a mantel, alongside some others that had been sent us from the church school children on Pitcairn Island. Hattie Andre was teaching there, and she had taught her pupils to make oil paintings of birds and flowers and scenery on large shells that they picked up along the seashore. The children had sent them to our father by the missionaries on the ship *Pitcairn*. He had passed them on to us.

In time our home became a gathering place for young people who came from Australia to receive missionary training at Battle Creek Sanitarium and College. One evening our guests noticed a wedding bell hanging in our bay window. Suddenly there was a lull in the chatter. Mr. Branstatter and Miss Grattidge had taken their places under the bell. Elder Tenny arose with solemn dignity and began plying the couple with serious questions. Their bashful "I do's" climaxed the evening's entertainment, and everybody was happy.

The socials held in our modest home on Kendall Street were simple affairs, with no extravagant outlay of money for entertainment or refreshments. I do remember that at one of the gatherings Mary served ice cream and home-baked cake. A report of the matter reached our father in Australia, with a criticism from a student in the school of health at the Sanitarium. Father wrote Mary that he was greatly pleased with the socials she was conducting for our friends, but for the sake of setting a good example, and upholding Dr. Kellogg in the reforms he was endeavoring to establish in healthful living, perhaps it would be better not to serve ice cream again.

In one of Papa's letters he told of visiting the ship *Pitcairn* when it docked for repairs at Napier, New Zealand, and of making a voyage along the New Zealand coast with the missionaries on board.

He wrote of a visit he made in company with Dr. Merritt Kellogg to the famous hot springs and hot lakes of New Zealand. There they watched the Maoris cook food in steam holes in the ground. The air was heavy with sulphurous fumes. Jets of steam rose from the ground on every side, and the guide warned sightseers to be careful where they stepped. Father and Dr. Kellogg saw two beautiful geysers shooting their crystal waters high into the air. Fascinated, they watched the water fall in glittering, rainbow-tinted spangles of indescribable beauty.

The group passed hot gushing geysers and boiling pools of black mud. At times there were loud boomings under their feet like the discharge of cannon; then up through the clear water of the river would rise a black, seething, viscous-looking column of mud. Things would quiet down; then in another minute the banging would begin again. The native people believed that in those grumbling, spluttering hot mud pools supper was being cooked for giants who had their abode beneath the mountains.

At the hotel where Papa and Dr. Kellogg lodged that night they were entertained with tales of frightening events that took place during the night of the eruption in 1886, events that created this weird wonderland.

On another occasion, while Papa and Grandma were spending a few days at the home of Joseph Hare at Kaeo, north New Zealand, they experienced a severe storm. The rain was so heavy that water poured down in torrents from the mountain slopes, carrying with it huge logs, parts of buildings, and scores of drowning sheep and cattle. The water rose until it was within sixteen inches of the floor of the house. In spite of all this excitement, however, Grandma was able to hold many meetings.

Sometimes Mabel and I would ask Mary to read Father's letters over several times. They were interesting, but we wondered why he didn't say something about coming home or about our going to Australia. Would our family always be separated?

Then one day the long-looked-for letter arrived. Papa wrote that Grandma's work was not finished in Australia. Since they would probably remain there for several more years, he was arranging for us girls to go to him. After a moment of silence, we clapped our hands and danced for joy.

"But let us finish reading the letter," said Mary. So she read on. In the letter Father told us a story we had never heard before. A few days before our mother's death she had called him to her bedside and told him that she hoped that after she was laid to rest he would find a good Christian woman whom he could love and who would help him make a home for himself and for his two little girls. Now at last he had found her. Her name was Ethel May Lacey, and she had been a Bible instructor. When Cousin May Walling had to return to America, May had come to care for Grandma and her large family. She had consented to be our mother, and he knew we would love her as he did. Now we could have a home all our own and be a happy little family again.

When Mary finished reading that letter Mabel and I were in tears. It was Mabel who spoke.

"Mary, why can't you be our mother instead of that other lady way over there?"

Then Mary's secret came out. She couldn't marry our papa even if he wanted her to. She had promised Elder George Tripp that she would marry him and help start a mission school in Africa. Also, she would be caring for his son, George, whose mother was dead and who needed a mamma just as much as we did.

Then Mary made us a proposition. If we would work and study hard and learn how to be good missionaries, in a few years she would send for us to come to Africa and help her teach the boys and girls in the mission school. That partially assuaged our grief, for we could look forward to seeing our dear Mary again.

And so it came about that in a few weeks Mabel and I said goodbye to Mary and our other friends in Battle Creek, and began a journey that would take us halfway round the world.

We made the long train trip to San Francisco in the care of Elder and

Mrs. F. J. Hutchins, who were returning to their mission field in the Bay Islands. In San Francisco they turned us over to Elder and Mrs. E. R. Palmer, who were on their way to Australia. Elder Palmer was going out to organize the colporteur work in the Australasian Mission Field, and would see that we reached there safe and sound.

To Australia

"We have prospects for a pleasant voyage," remarked Elder Palmer as he helped Mabel and me stow our suitcases and blanket rolls under our bunks. The Palmers and their 6-month-old baby, Pansy, occupied the two berths on one side of the cabin. Mabel had the top berth on the other side, and I the lower one.

"And, look," I exclaimed, "our porthole opens onto the lower deck! We can keep it open all the time without any danger of getting a salt-water shower bath." I could not conceal my delight.

We had no time for the cabin now, but bounded up onto the deck to join the crowd at the rail, waving hats and handkerchiefs. The dinner bell rang, but who wanted to stop to eat and miss the last fading sight of our dear America? We watched as the Golden Gate city and the shoreline became dimmer and dimmer, until the scene finally melted into the horizon, leaving nothing but blue sky and blue water above, below, beyond, surrounding us on all sides.

For all of the first day and part of the second, great white gulls followed the ship, their powerful wings spread wide as they dived for scraps of food thrown overboard from the ship's kitchens.

"How can they stay up in the air so long? Don't they ever stop to rest?" I asked one of the sailors.

"Oh, yes," he answered. "At night they transform their bodies from flying boats into seaworthy sailing vessels. They tuck their heads under their folded wings and sleep, floating on the surface of the water. Their closely packed oily feathers keep the living seacrafts waterproof, and they rest at ease."

The third day out the gulls left our vessel to attach themselves to one bound shoreward, leaving the porpoises as our ship's only traveling companions. Hour after hour these remarkable creatures swam alongside the steamer, as if challenging it to a race.

Now and then, schools of flying fish leaped from the water, their fin-wings glistening as if sprinkled with diamond dust. After a brief moment they quickly dropped from sight again beneath the surface. In the evenings we enjoyed standing at the stern of the vessel, fascinated by the phosphorescent waves of light churned up by the propeller. The glistening cascades thus created fed a shining stream that rested on the surface of the water in the ship's wake, and seemed to reach nearly to the horizon. We were told that the sparkle was due to millions of phosphorescent jellyfish.

Another enjoyable pastime was watching the sailors scramble up to the top of the mastheads. They seemed as quick as monkeys, never making a misstep or losing their footing. And there was the great engine to watch, and the firemen down in the furnace room, stoking the flames that heated the water, that made the steam, that moved the pistons, that worked the machinery, that moved the great ship over the water, carrying us to our new home on the other side of the world.

In the evenings there were entertainments in the dining salon with singing and music, and sometimes impromptu programs by the passengers, to which Mabel and I contributed musical selections or recitations of poetry.

Much of the time Mrs. Palmer was too seasick to take care of Baby Pansy, and Mr. Palmer was more accustomed to making and selling books than to tending infants. But that all pleased Mabel immensely. She gloried in her favorite occupation as nursemaid. At her request, Brother Palmer would spread a blanket on the deck floor, carry the baby up the gangway, and commit her to Mabel's care for the day.

We were to stop at Hawaii, and after nearly six days of smooth sailing, we were awakened one morning by the cry "Land in sight!" It took only the proverbial jiffy for us to rush up on deck, where we could watch the dim outline take definite shape and grow larger and larger, until palm trees and cottages were visible against a background of green hills.

We drew up at the Honolulu dock and were soon surrounded on all sides by brown children splashing about in the water and shouting, "Penny, penny, penny!" Coins were flung over the side of the ship, and *splash!* all heads disappeared. Then came happy shouts from one direction and another as the children bobbed to the surface. The winners held their captured trifles high above their heads for an instant, then popped them into their mouths and called for more. So the fun went on, with a steady accumulation of dimes, quarters, sixpences, and shillings. Steamer days were days well improved by the resourceful youngsters of Honolulu.

While the vessel rested, uniformed bands gathered on the wharf and treated the passengers to a concert of festive national songs with guitar and ukelele accompaniments. The musicians presented a romantic scene, but not more so than did the beautiful Hawaiian women, barefoot, in brightly colored silk gowns, gorgeously festooned with garlands of flowers.

Mrs. Kerr, the wife of a prosperous businessman, and an Adventist, sent her carriage and brought our party to her home, where a banquet was set out for us. Next there was an impressive service at the little Adventist church. All too soon the steamer's shrill whistle announced that it was time for departure.

Another six days aboard ship brought us to our next stopping place, the island of Samoa. Here the steamer was unable to dock, because of a dangerous coral reef. From our anchorage in the bay, we saw a score of native canoes coming rapidly toward us. They were paddled by scantily clad Samoans, many of whom appeared to be wearing white nightcaps. Ropes were slung over the side of the ship and the rowers clambered up, hand over hand, drawing baskets of fruit and curios with them. Then business began.

A basket of six dozen oranges was sold for a shilling (about 24 cents at the time), and a bunch of bananas cost little more. Close inspection proved that some of the men had their heads plastered with a thick covering of lime, which had given us the illusion of white nightcaps when seen at a distance. The lime turned their glossy black hair to a faded red, which was decreed by the beauty specialists in that locality to be the height of fashion. Their bodies were covered with paint and tattoo marks and weighted with earrings, nose rings, bracelets, armlets, and leglets, all made of brass.

While the men carried on a brisk trade in fruit, curios, coral, and basketwares, some of the women amused the passengers with native dances. With remarkable agility the younger women went through their fantastic movements, while the grandmas and children sat on the deck floor clapping their hands and tapping an accompaniment with their feet.

We would gladly have spent three days instead of three hours in this romantic spot. But the whistle was blowing. The natives gathered up their now-empty baskets, clambered down into their canoes, and paddled for the shore.

On Monday, after our stop at Samoa, we crossed the dateline and lived two days in one. Here we parted with the North Star and its friendly family, the Big Dipper, and with many other star friends. We had reached the "other side of the world" and would now make the acquaintance of the Southern Cross. One night the ship's steward pointed out a particularly brilliant star at every point of the Cross where Jesus was wounded—at His head, where the crown of thorns pierced His temples, one at each point, where nails were driven through His outstretched hands, one at the left side, where the spear thrust was received, and a double star at His feet.

The last stop on our long journey was at Auckland, New Zealand. Here we were entertained by Brother and Sister Edward Hare and taken to interesting spots in the city and to Mount Eden, an extinct volcano with a crater extending about one half the depth of the mountain.

On our first day out from Auckland we ran into a real storm. How our ship rolled and pitched and tossed! At times the propeller was lifted out of the water, causing the entire vessel to shiver from stem to stern. Waves rose mountain high—so it seemed to us—and broke in torrents over the deck. Lightning flashed almost continuously, and thunder boomed close behind. At times our ship would be riding high on the crest, and the next moment we would drop down, down, down into a trough between the huge waves. The movements were most severe in the stern, where our cabin was situated.

To prevent being rolled around too violently, Mabel crawled into the bunk with me, and we wedged a blanket from her upper berth between us. That night all the lights went out, and we were in total darkness.

There were a number of pets aboard, and during the storm they set up a terror concert. A parrot in a cage just outside our deck window began screeching, a dog howled, and somebody's pet monkey screamed incessantly. The vocalizing continued through most of the night, finally quieting down enough to enable us to catch a few winks of sleep before daylight.

In the morning Mabel and I left our bunks and half walked, half crawled along the passageway to the dining salon. As we entered, the piano at one end of the room was thrown first one way then the other. Finally, it fell over with a bang that threatened to smash it to kindling wood. At breakfast, little frames were placed around our dishes to prevent them from sliding. Waiters carrying breakfast trays walked slowly and unsteadily. We saw one of them slip and fall. Only the hardiest passengers ventured on deck or to the dining room.

The storm continued for three days, becoming less severe, until on the fourth day it settled into comparative calm. Early on the fifth day we heard the now familiar cry "Land in sight!" A more welcome sound we had never heard, and all who were able to stand rushed onto the deck to watch the shoreline as we entered beautiful Sydney harbor.

Verdure extended for miles along the banks of both sides as we slowly made our way through the narrow opening and up the bay, passing two old stone forts and two lighthouses. Beyond were grassy hills adorned with splendid residences. Yonder was Woolloomooloo Bay, where several warships lay at anchor. Trading boats, flying the flags of many nations, sailed in and out among the larger vessels. We steamed past Government House, the Botanical Gardens, and the city park. Then, quickly rounding a point, we drew up at the wharf.

Soon the deck was a scene of noisy activity—chains rattling, trunks and boxes being moved about, officers and sailors shouting to one another. While Brother Palmer strapped up bundles and closed suitcases, Mabel dropped a few salty tears as she sat down on a bedding roll to hold Baby Pansy for the last time. When would she see the darling little girl again?

I was scanning the crowds gathered on the wharf, searching for a woman dressed in gray carrying a gray purse. She would be looking for two little girls in blue sailor suits and caps.

Presently I saw a gray purse waving. Three seconds and my cap was off and I was waving a happy response.

GRANDMA'S HOME

The lady in gray was Emily Campbell, one of Grandma's office helpers. She steered Mabel and me through customs and out to a carriage where Marian Davis was waiting to greet us. It gave me a real at-home feeling to see my old friend again. I remembered Miss Davis from our days in Europe, where she had often saved her pencils for me to scribble with when they got too short for her to use.

An hour's drive brought us to Norfolk Villa, Grandma's temporary home in Granville, a suburb of Sydney. There was scarcely time to lay off our wraps and wash up before the dinner bell rang and Miss Campbell ushered us into the dining room.

"Oh, what a long table!" exclaimed Mabel in a loud whisper. She counted the plates. Miss Campbell smiled.

"The table isn't as long as it usually is," she explained. "As you know, your father and grandmother and Miss Lacey are away attending meetings in Victoria. Before they return they will stop at Miss Lacey's home in Hobart, Tasmania, where your papa and new mamma will get married."

We were ready to eat. Never shall I forget that dinner. Those fluffy baked potatoes and just-a-bit-crunchy cauliflower! The fresh ripe tomatoes and home-baked whole-wheat bread spread with honey and rich cream! Mabel sat across the table from me, and a big bowl of cream was placed between us with the invitation, "Help yourselves, girls." And after four weeks of existing on ship's fare, be assured that we did just that. We were told that Grandma kept a Jersey cow and used the thick cream skimmed from pans of boiled milk in place of butter, which was sold in grocery stores from open jars and was not always fresh and wholesome.

With my hunger partly assuaged, I began to take note of our surroundings and to pay a little courteous attention to our introductions. The girl at my right was Edith Ward. Her mother was dead, and she had come to live in Grandma's family. I was delighted, for she was about my own age. We immediately made friends with our eyes. Across the table next to Mabel, was another little girl, Nettie Hamilton, just two years older than Mabel, and beside her sat her mother, a tiny dot of a woman not much bigger than Nettie herself.

Acting as host in Father's absence was a pleasant-faced gentleman named Caldwell. Seventeen-year-old Willie McCann sat at the end of the table. We were told that Willie was an indispensable member of the family. He took care of the garden, the chickens, also the horse and cow, and kept things around the place looking spick and span. Miss Davis was seated at the opposite end of the table. Miss Campbell was there, of course, and one or two others.

While we were eating, Annie Ulrick, a German girl, came in to wait on table, and in explanation, Miss Campbell remarked, "We can never persuade Annie to sit down and eat with us."

"Because servant girls never do so in my country," spoke up Annie, and, blushing, she quickly disappeared into the kitchen.

After dinner, while Edith and Nettie were washing the dishes, Miss Davis took Mabel and me upstairs to her room.

"My bedroom has to serve as my workroom, also," she explained, as she opened her door and revealed her bedroom floor almost entirely covered with sheets of typewritten paper.

"These are selections from your grandmother's writings that are going into a new book on the life of Christ. I think she has written more about the life of Jesus than about anyone or anything else in the whole world. It is her favorite theme. But, with all her public work and travels and her crowded program, it is difficult for her to sit down and give her undivided attention to writing the book. She has written some complete chapters, but in other places there are gaps in the story.

"So she asked me to go through her published articles and sermons, as well as her letters and diaries, and copy out the best things she has written about the life and teachings of Jesus, and bring them into the book to fill out the incomplete chapters. I've spent months doing this, and I've found whole pages of precious material that should go into the book, and many paragraphs and sentences that will fill in some of the missing details in the story. My work saves your grandmother much time and makes it possible for her to do more writing."

She paused, and I remarked, "How wonderful that you can help Grandma write her books!"

"Oh, no!" Miss Davis answered quickly. "I never do any of the writing. Your grandma writes her own books. She writes what God tells her to write. None of us ever add anything to what she writes. One time one of the typists did change some of the manuscripts she was copying. She thought she could make your grandma's plain, simple language more flowery and attractive. But when your grandmother read it over, she changed it all back again the way she had written it; and then she found another kind of work for that lady to do."

Mabel and I listened soberly as Miss Davis told us more about what she did to help our grandmother. Part of my work is to see that the spelling and punctuation are correct, and that the paragraphs are arranged in the correct order in the chapters and the chapters are given the right titles, and to see that there is no repetition.

"When everything is in order, the whole manuscript is copied again. Then your grandmother gives it a final reading.

"Those pages you see spread out on the floor are part of a chapter she has written for the book on the life of Jesus. While I was reading through one of her articles I found some lovely things that she wrote on the same subject that ought to go into this chapter. Now I must find the right places to fit these new selections into the story. Your grandma wrote it all, but at different times."

There was a knock on the door, and Nettie called, "Mabel and Ella, my mamma wants to take us for a walk. Edith is coming too."

Down the garden path we skipped, following our leader, we two newcomers pausing now and then to admire some new variety of flower we had never seen before. It was a mild day in April, though the country was getting ready for winter, which in the Southern Hemisphere comes during what are the summer months in the North. We four girls sat down on the grassy hillside and pulled off our shoes and stockings. How good the soft, cool grass felt to our bare feet!

Before Mrs. Hamilton had time to open her handbag and take out the story paper she had brought along to read to us, Mabel and I began

asking questions. For one thing, we wanted to know how Edith and
Nettie came to be living in Grandma's home and whether we would
have them for playmates permanently.

"Oh, yes," Edith said. "Your grandma says that I am to stay here in
her home until the Avondale boarding school opens. Then she'll send
me and my brother Ernest to the school home. It's going to take a year or
two to put up the school buildings so we shall have a nice long time
together.

"When your grandmother heard what a hard time we were having
trying to get along without Mother, she hunted us up and asked how I
would like to come and be her little girl for a while. She put her arm
around me and looked so loving and kind that I said, 'Yes, I would.'
That's why I am here."

"And she hunted us up, too," added Mrs. Hamilton. "When Nettie's
father died 'way over in Scotland, I took Nettie with me, and we came to
Australia. I set up a dressmaking and millinery shop in Sydney. My
business prospered, and I sent for my sister and older daughter to join
us. But the ship on which they sailed was lost at sea, and Nettie and I
were left alone in Sydney.

"Then came several years of depression, and people had little
money to spend for the pretty things we made. I had to close my shop.
About that time Nettie and I attended some Bible lectures and learned
that the seventh day of the week, Saturday, and not the first day, Sunday,
is the true Sabbath. The seventh day is the day God blessed and
commanded everyone to keep holy. Work was hard to obtain, especially
for those who refused to work on Saturday, the busiest day of the week.

"Nettie and I decided to keep God's day, even if we had to starve for
doing so. But we really believed that God would take care of us.

"Then, what do you think happened? Your grandmother heard of
the difficulty we were in and came to see us.

" 'How would you and Nettie like to join my family of helpers?' she
asked. 'My two little granddaughters will soon arrive from America. That
will make four little girls in our home, and you can be their governness.
You can teach them dressmaking and millinery; and you can do the
sewing for my family of workers.' "

When Nettie's mother finished speaking there was silence for a moment. Then we asked, "What about Willie?" All of us liked him, and Mrs. Hamilton smiled as she told his story.

"Willie McCann has eight brothers and sisters at home. That is a large family to provide for, especially in these hard times. His father began keeping the Bible Sabbath about the same time that Nettie and I did. His faith has been tested just as ours was. He lost a good position and had to depend on odd jobs for the support of his family. Work was scarce and hard to secure in times of depression.

"Mrs. McCann stood right by her husband, and together they decided that they would obey God even if they had to suffer for their faith. When your grandmother learned that the family was in actual need of food she didn't wait for them to come to her for help. Instead, she went at once to the grocery store and bought supplies and took them to Willie's home.

"While they were talking and praying together, Willie came into the room and your grandma asked about him. Then she turned to the boy.

" 'Willie,' she said, 'how would you like to be my garden boy and take care of the horse and cow and chickens and keep the place in order?' So that's what Willie is doing. Your grandmother pays him sufficient to keep the family from dire want until Mr. McCann can find steady employment. Willie doesn't mind my telling this. He himself tells his friends how good Mrs. White has been to him."

"And Annie? What about Annie?" we asked next. We were really getting acquainted with Grandma's family. Mrs. Hamilton took up her story again.

"When Annie became a Seventh-day Adventist her parents were so angry because she had left her former church and joined such an unpopular people as the Seventh-day Adventists that they turned her out of the house.

"Your grandmother didn't really need any more helpers just then, but there was one job left that she could give Annie to do. There was no one in the house officially appointed as cook. Would Annie do the cooking?

" 'But, Mrs. White,' Annie protested, 'I've never been anything but a chambermaid. I don't know how to cook.' The poor girl was embarrassed.

" 'Never mind, Annie; we'll show you how to cook.' So Annie came, and now she is learning fast."

Then we wanted to know about the kind-faced man who was acting as our host while Papa was away; and so we had another story.

"Well," began Mrs. Hamilton, "Mr. Caldwell came from America on a mission that he thought was very important. But Adventist people in Australia didn't support him or his mission. He found himself stranded far from home, without money and without friends. Your grandmother knew that he was honest and conscientious, but just a bit mixed up in his head. She felt sorry for him. So she gave him a home and some odd jobs to keep him busy. Now he is better, and ready to go back to his home again.

"I suppose you would like to know about the two ladies who were at the table today. They help with the office work, typing your grandmother's letters, articles, and sermons and copying her book manuscripts."

I was beginning to think that what Nettie's mother said about Grandma was true; and I was very sure of it after I had lived in her family for a time. I never knew my grandmother to turn any persons away if she could possibly help them—not so long as there was room at the table for another plate or a corner in the house where an extra cot could be set up.

Three weeks after Mabel and I arrived in Australia our father, with his lovely English bride, came from Tasmania. With love and tenderness Ethel May Lacey White opened her arms and her heart to us motherless girls. I was 13 and Mabel 8. We hadn't seen Father for four years. After the greetings, he took the team and went to the station for the luggage. On his way back, he saw his bride walking along the road with two young girls, one on each side holding her hands. Father sprang from the wagon, knelt on the path beside us, and enclosed the three of us in one big bear hug. At last we were a family again!

Cooranbong

While living in Grandma's home in Granville, Mabel and I heard much about a nearly fifteen-hundred-acre tract of land that had been purchased for the purpose of establishing the Australasian Missionary Training School. One day early in July (midwinter in Australia) Father and Mother and Grandma boarded a northbound train, taking Mabel and me with them. We were on our way to Cooranbong, a village situated on the borders of the new school property.

Mother's family, the Laceys, had moved over from Tasmania and rented a cottage in Cooranbong village, so that they might be near the school when it opened. They invited our family to share the cottage with them. This we were glad to do.

Every morning at about five o'clock Father and Grandma walked across a plot of grass to an old hotel building that temporarily housed about thirty young men who were beginning to clear the school property. Mabel and I and the young Laceys often went with them to listen to Grandma's inspiring talks of faith and to hear Father discuss plans with Professor L. J. Rousseau, the director of the school.

The young men had come to work up credit for their future schooling. During the daylight hours they worked on the land, grubbing out trees and stumps, clearing away underbrush, draining swamps, building roads, fencing land, and preparing a site for the school buildings and ground for orchard and garden.

The old hotel building served temporarily for both dormitory and classroom. In the evening, with the day's work finished and supper out of the way, school books were brought forth and the hotel dining room was transformed into an institution of learning. It was an inspiration for Father and Grandmother to talk to those young men, who were so eager to gain a Christian education that they were willing to work hard for it.

Grandma decided to make Avondale her permanent home. She

bought forty acres of forest land adjacent to the school property and moved onto the grounds, so that she might supervise the erection of her home and the planting of an orchard. A small cookhouse was built, and a number of tents were set up to accommodate the workmen, as well as herself. Mrs. Maude Camp was engaged as cook.

After a stay of a few weeks at Cooranbong, Mother and Father returned to Granville to get ready for the move to Avondale. Mabel returned with them, but I stayed as a companion for Grandma, and shared her tent. I remember sometimes waking in the early mornings and parting the curtains that separated my corner of the tent from her living quarters. I would see her sitting in her armchair, with a lapboard across her knees, writing by the light of a kerosene lamp.

There were many interesting things for a 13-year-old girl to see and do. It was fun helping Maude Camp serve meals in the dining tent. It was even more fun to drive around the countryside with Grandma when she went to order supplies for the carpenters, or fruit trees and berry plants for her orchard. At that time Grandma was 67. She would often let me drive the horses for her, and I thought it great fun.

Once we went in search of a good cow. We purchased Molly and brought her home and turned her loose in our enclosed pasture. A task that I remember with much pleasure was going with Grandma to get Molly at milking time in the evening. I would let down the bars that served as a temporary gate to the pasture enclosure, and we would walk down the path toward the school site. Then, at the sound of the bell around Molly's neck, I would shout and flourish my stick to start the cow moving, while Grandma stood on the path calling, "Co, Boss! Co, Boss!"

October 1, 1896, was a truly notable day in the history of Avondale College. Money had been loaned to Grandma for the immediate erection of some buildings. A gathering was called for the purpose of laying the foundation stone (which was really a brick). Grandma White with pleasure took the trowel and performed the task. As she looked around on the downcast countenances of the group before her, she said happily, "Cheer up, children; this is a resurrection, not a funeral."

Building operations on my grandmother's house progressed slowly because of the extreme hardness of the wood with which the carpenters were building. But on Christmas Day she, with two or three of her helpers, moved into the unfinished home, which was named Sunnyside.

The remainder of our large family arrived a few at a time, some by train and some by wagon, bringing furniture and livestock with them. We four girls—Edith, Nettie, Mabel, and I—had glorious times roaming the woods together, chasing wallabies (a small species of kangaroo), transplanting ferns and wildflowers from the forest to our home gardens, and wading in the pond.

After living in Grandma's home for a few weeks, Father, Mother, Mabel, and I set up housekeeping for ourselves in a small building intended ultimately for storage and laundry. We were barely settled in our temporary living quarters in time to welcome our twin brothers. When we were presented with two babies instead of the one we had expected we girls danced for joy. Mabel gave away both of her dolls and promptly assumed the roll of nursemaid, giving me scarcely a chance to look at the twins, Henry and Herbert. It was fortunate that I had other interests or there might have been friction.

Fanny Bolton, who was returning to America, gave us her riding pony as a parting gift. Myrtle trotted along so fast on her short little legs that even riding bareback was almost like floating through the air. Mabel and I spent many a pleasant afternoon exploring the countryside, sitting astride Myrtle.

One day Edith and I went for a fifteen-mile horseback ride with Iram James, Grandma's farm manager, who was getting some choice grapevines for planting in her vineyard. He told us not to take lunch, and we wondered why. Arriving at the vineyard, we were invited to enter and eat all the grapes we wanted. They were a delicious variety, much like the California muscats. We were glad then that we had not filled up on sandwiches.

Grandma's orchard and garden thrived. One of the first things she instructed Mr. James to do was to clear, fence, and fertilize a piece of ground and seed it to alfalfa. This would contribute to the health of her cows (she now had two). We could drink all the good, rich milk we wanted, and we could eat all the oranges and other fruit we could hold.

Once a week, on bake days, we would gather dry fuel from the woods and make a hot fire inside the Dutch oven that Grandma had ordered built from brick and mortar. When the coals were red-hot, we would rake them out and wipe out the oven with a damp mop. Then in went the bread, thirteen or fourteen large pans at a time. When the golden-brown loaves came out we would have six or eight apple or peach pies ready to go in, and while they were baking we would slice up two or three loaves of bread ready to pop into the slowly cooling oven when the pies came out. With bread, zwieback, pies, and an abundance of fresh fruit and vegetables, and milk from the farm, our two families lived well with little trouble or expense.

While our branch of the family was occupying the storage-laundry building, our weekly wash was done at a pond on the lower end of the property. Mother initiated Mabel and me to the task. After a few weeks' experience we volunteered to take over the entire responsibility for the family washing.

First the white things were scrubbed and put into a big copper boiler. While they were boiling we scrubbed the coloreds, rinsed them, and hung them on the line. Then we would suds, rinse, and blue the whites and hang them out. Sometimes the clothes got an extra long boiling while we watched, fascinated, as a mother platypus that had her home in the pond gave her babies a swimming lesson.

When our chore was finished Mabel and I would race home, for we knew a good dinner was waiting for us; there was always something extra on washdays.

Winter was coming on, so Father rented an eight-room house in Cooranbong. The place was known as the Convent, because some nuns had once lived and worked there. Mother's brother Herbert and his wife, Lillian, came to board with us. After completing their education at Battle Creek and Healdsburg colleges, respectively, they had been appointed to teach at the Avondale school. Lenora, one of Mother's younger sisters, joined us and shared the housework. We also cared for an old gentleman in his 80s who was in the custody of the school board. So we had quite a large family. Besides this, our house became a sort of wayside inn for itinerant ministers and a place where council and committee meetings were held. Not infrequently it was necessary to add the kitchen table to the one in the dining room in order to seat all our dinner guests. There was plenty of work for all of us.

Mother's time was occupied largely in caring for the twins, supervising the home, entertaining guests, and sewing for the family. Lenora and I shared the household duties, taking turns with the cooking and general housework. It was there in that old convent building that I received my first schooling in real work.

The rough, unpainted board floors required frequent scrubbing. Our ancient wood-burning stove on which we did our cooking and baking had a crack across the top. How that stove smoked as we stuffed in the green eucalyptus wood that Father salvaged from the clearings on the college grounds!

Dishwater had to be carried into the house in buckets from a well outside. It was heated on the back of the stove, and the dishes were washed in a pan on the kitchen table. On bath day two corrugated iron washtubs were taken upstairs to the bedrooms, and warm water was carried up in buckets. Other housekeeping operations were performed on an equally primitive level.

Mabel's responsibility was caring for the lighting system of the establishment—fifteen kerosene lamps. Every day they had to be trimmed and filled and the glass globes washed and polished. Frequently, just about the time Mabel was well started on the task, she would be attracted to the front door by the shouting of teamsters and the cracking of whips. With a lamp globe in one hand and a towel in the other, she would stand and watch the line of bullock-drawn lumber wagons, loaded with logs from the mountains, pass by the house. There were usually two or three wagons in the procession, each drawn by a team of twelve or sixteen bullocks. Down the road they would come, past the grocery store, the blacksmith shop, our house, and on to the sawmill a few miles down the road. Lamp cleaning waited until the excitement was over, but before dinner time the lamps all stood in a row on the kitchen shelf, waiting for members of the family to carry them to their respective rooms. Mabel was happy at the completion of the job for there was nothing else for her to do the rest of the day but play with the babies.

While we were living at the Convent, a tent was pitched nearby for a month-long teacher and ministerial institute. Some of the village people came out to the evening meetings, and after the institute closed Elder George B. Starr gave a series of Bible lectures particularly for them. I remember how energetically I practiced the hymns selected beforehand, so that I might have the honor of being organist on our portable four-octave organ. On several occasions after the discourse, Father gave a short, friendly talk, telling the village people about the school we were planning to establish among them and inviting them to send their young folk there to obtain a Christian education.

Constable Berry, at the police station a few rods down the road from the Convent, told my father that he could not have chosen a worse place in which to establish a school. Just over the mountains, he said, there was a community of 250 descendants of three convict families sent out in the early days from England. Some of them had settled in Cooranbong, and he warned us that nothing was too hot or too heavy for them to carry away. We found this to be true. Food prepared for Sabbath dinner at our home and set in the milk house behind the Convent disappeared overnight—dishes, pans, and all. Marauders scouted as far as Grandma's orchard and vegetable garden. Provisions were stolen from her shed.

I might say, in confirmation of Grandma's common sense, however, that she instructed her farm manager to secure a vigilant watchdog. Tiglath-pileser was a terror to evildoers. But he was never kept near the house, lest his barking frighten children or interfere with the coming and going of visitors.

In spite of a serious shortage of funds and a period of national depression, work on the Avondale school estate continued to make progress, under the competent management of Metcalf Hare and the help of students attending the industrial night school. Grubbing out those mammoth trees with mattock and spade was no small task. Many were the blisters produced in the process before the stumps were gone, the underbrush cleared away, and the land broken open by oxen and plows.

The school sawmill continued to operate faithfully, transforming trees into timber for the erection of school buildings. When there was an interruption in milling operations because of shortage of money with which to operate the machinery the sawmill team joined the other industrial students in the ever-present task of clearing land, plowing, planting, cultivating, and setting out orchard and vineyard.

The outgoing mail to America carried frequent appeals from Grandma to conferences, churches, and old acquaintances for money with which to advance the school project. Our father and Elder Daniells visited the young churches in Australia and New Zealand, appealing to members to invest in the school, either by gifts or by loans. They promised that when school was opened it would no longer be necessary to send young men and women across the Pacific to obtain missionary training in America.

For months building was delayed for lack of money. Then Grandma arranged to borrow some money from Mrs. Wessels in Africa, and with this the buildings were begun. When the funds arrived, plans were immediately made for the laying of the cornerstone before Grandma would embark on a trip to Sydney and Melbourne for camp meeting.

By this time Cousin May Walling had returned to America, and Sara McEnterfer, who had been detained by illness when Grandma's party left for Australia, now joined the working staff at Sunnyside. When Grandma was at home, Sara would take her for a ride in her horse-drawn carriage nearly every afternoon. In the homes they visited they sometimes found distressing cases of sickness. Many of the patients they treated made such a rapid recovery, under proper diet and treatment, that it was soon a matter of common remark that Adventists knew how to cure the sick and that they were always ready to help those in need. It was hinted that perhaps their religion was not as bad as some of the ministers and priests had intimated. Little by little the people became our friends. Thieving ceased, drunkards became sober, pipes were discarded, and real conversions took place.

On Sabbath afternoons students went out from the school on bicycles, holding Bible studies in homes scattered throughout the surrounding forests and villages, or conducting branch Sabbath-schools. If an audience could not be gathered on the Sabbath day, then a Sunday school would be held. Grandma would release some members of her office staff and send them out with her horse and carriage to assist the students in conducting Sunday Bible classes.

Every week a group of students took a rowboat and paddled four miles down Dora Creek to conduct Sabbath school and church service in a rented cottage in a fishing village. It was there that I taught my first class of rosy-cheeked, barefoot children.

At Martinsville I had the fun of helping to clean and whitewash a discarded henhouse and equip it as a Sabbath school room. It was a little crowded, so in fair weather primary and junior classes recited outdoors on the grass. We knew that angels of God were as willing to meet with us in those humble surroundings as in the most splendid cathedrals and churches. We were happy.

A Timely Message

Many of the heavenly messages communicated through Ellen White were addressed to ministers and church leaders, teachers, Bible instructors, and physicians, but not all. Some were for young people and children and the other church members. Once, when I was 14 years old and Mabel was 9, Grandma White was given a testimony especially for our family, and most of it was addressed particularly to me.

Lenora and I were attending the night industrial school, which had been transferred from the old hotel building in Cooranbong to the new loft erected over the sawmill. Every evening at about six o'clock, Lenora and I, with Herbert and Lillian Lacey and the younger members of the Lacey family, would pick up our lanterns and, single file, traipse down the narrow path through the woods to the school site. We would climb the steep, narrow stairs on the outside of the building to the loft floor, there to sit on plank benches and recite our lessons by lantern light, along with the young men working on the school property.

One night when I returned with the others from our evening classes I was tired and discouraged. There was so much work to do and so little time for study. I flung myself on the bed and gave way to grief and tears. But the old habit of taking my troubles to God in prayer prevailed.

"O God, dear God," I pleaded, "give me strength to go on. Take away my bitter feelings and let me know the peace I once enjoyed." But I seemed to find no relief in prayer. It didn't seem as if I were talking to God at all, or as if He were anywhere near. I prayed on and on for a long time, but felt no assurance of His presence. Finally, feeling utterly forsaken, I lay down with a lonesome ache in my heart. After some time, I fell into a troubled sleep.

It may have been the next day—at least very soon after this, as I remember—that Grandma's carriage stopped at the Convent door. She did not greet us with her usual cheery "Good afternoon," but said very seriously, "Willie, call your family together; I have words to speak to them." She always called our father Willie.

We came into the front room—Father, Mother, Mabel, and I, with our little twin brothers. As usual, Mabel picked up Baby Henry and I took Herbert on my lap.

Grandma said, "Will someone take care of the twins? I want Ella and Mabel to give me all their attention, for I have a solemn message for them."

When we were quietly seated, she opened the small satchel in which she carried her writings and took out a manuscript written that morning. There was absolute silence as she began reading it to us.

"I was unable to sleep after eleven o'clock. In the night season I had been instructed of God. I have been made to feel deeply. One stood in our midst. Willie, his wife, May, and several others were present. Words of deep import were spoken."

First, several sentences were addressed to our parents. They were told that our household was too large; there was too much noise and confusion in the home, too much forgetfulness of God in daily duties. There should be more time for Bible study. We children must be taught to form orderly habits, to keep our clothes clean and mended. How I hated mending! I lost a sentence or two thinking about it. Bringing my thoughts back, I listened more carefully.

"Let a living faith run like threads of gold through the daily experiences, in the performance of little duties. 'Whatsoever ye do, do all to the glory of God.' Then there will be a looking unto Jesus; love for Him will be the continual motive, giving vital force to everything that is undertaken."

Words were then addressed directly to us girls: "Your mother needs your help as members of the firm. Be true to home duties. Take heed to her counsel and instruction. Respect her words. Obey her requests. This is a part of your education that will fit you to become members of the family above."

As Grandma continued, I realized that most of the testimony was meant especially for us. My name was mentioned several times. I was told that my work was to set a right example before my younger sister by being a living Christian, faithful in all the little home duties, heeding every suggestion mother made, yet not waiting for her to tell me what to do when I myself could see what needed to be done.

I should keep my room in order, carefully removing all dust and dirt. The kitchen was to be kept neat and clean.

Interrupting Grandma, I asked, "Did the angel say all those things, or did you think of them yourself as you were writing?"

Grandma replied, "The angel talked with me in the night; and while it was yet dark, I arose and dressed and wrote down the messages that were given to me for you and Mabel and your parents."

Then she read on: "Books are to be laid aside for their proper season, and no more study should engross the mind than can be attended to without neglecting the household duties. You may fill your place in the household as a thoughtful, care-taking, practical Christian, working for Jesus, doing the little duties that are often disagreeble but which must be done and not delayed."

We were told not to be discouraged. Angels were watching to see how they could work with us to help us develop Christlike characters. Then, lifting Mabel to her lap, Grandma put her arm around me as she read the last words of the testimony.

"In doing your daily duties promptly, neatly, faithfully, you are missionaries. You are bearing witness for Christ. You are showing that the religion of Christ does not, in principle or practice, make you untidy, coarse, disrespectful to your parents by taking little heed to their counsel and instruction. Bible religion practiced will make you kind, thoughtful, faithful. You will not neglect the little things that should be done to give a neat, wholesome appearance even in the kitchen. . . . 'He that is faithful in that which is least is faithful also in much.'"

Grandma finished reading. She laid the manuscript in Mother's hands and stood up.

I immediately fled upstairs to my room, buried my face in the pillow, and cried. My thoughts were bitter and resentful. Why did I have to spend so much time sweeping and scrubbing and washing dishes? I needed time for study. That was one reason I had been discouraged and blue. I wanted to stand high in my night school classes. Then, suddenly, as if struck by lightning, I remembered my prayer. So very recently, I had knelt in that same spot and asked God for help. Was this His answer?

Had the great God in heaven heard the cry of a young girl and sent an angel with the answer to her request? Yes, God had heard me. He *did* love me! He had sent this message of reproof *because* He loved me!

Tears of repentance took the place of the wicked, rebellious tears of a few moments before. I knelt where I had so recently prayed in despair. God had *not* forsaken me!

As soon as I could wash away the tearstains, I hurried down to the room where Father, Mother, and Mabel were talking together. Grandma had gone. I threw myself into Mother's arms.

"Ella," Father said tenderly, "you have had a hard time these past months. Life has not been easy for any of us. But these trials will pass. Soon we shall be living in our cottage, just us four with the twins and Joe. We'll not have so large a family to care for nor so many visitors to entertain.

"There will be no more rough board floors to scrub. We'll have a new cookstove, not like this old, cracked one that smokes up the kitchen. The green eucalyptus branches that I have been salvaging from the clearing shall have had time to dry out and will burn better."

"And we'll have a bathroom, won't we, Papa, with a bathtub?" Mabel volunteered happily. "We won't have to carry the water and the tub upstairs anymore!"

Mother pressed my hand. "Think of it, Ella; there will be a sink in the kitchen and water on tap from a big tank outside. And Joe Mills will be here to help us. Even though he is only 15 years old, he is willing and clever, and can take care of us while Father is away. He can make the garden and help around the house."

"And milk the cow," I announced emphatically, thinking of another burden that would be rolled off my shoulders.

"And I shall have only half as many lamps to take care of," said Mabel jubilantly.

For some minutes I had been thinking about a sticky saucepan I had left soaking, well hidden behind the kitchen stove. As soon as I could be sure no one was looking, I took it to the sandpile behind the house and gave it a good scouring. Then I looked around the kitchen, straightened things up here and there, threw out a half-rotten pumpkin, and energetically scrubbed the table.

" 'He that is faithful in that which is least is faithful also in much,' " I repeated to myself. "Hereafter I shall try to do every task as faithfully and carefully as if I could look up and see Jesus standing nearby, observing everything I am doing."

It was not long after this that we moved into our new house across the road from Grandma's home.

A Medical Mission at Avondale

The Avondale School for Christian Workers was formally opened on April 28, 1897. In the rush of finishing the building, every able-bodied person in the community was given the opportunity of helping. Iram James laid the floorboards while Mrs. Haskell and Miss McEnterfer pounded in the nails. We younger folk followed along after the builders, cleaning paint off the windows and removing plaster from the floors.

Part of the dining room was divided by temporary partitions into two classrooms. In one of these small rooms Mrs. C. B. Hughes, the principal's wife, instructed a class in grammar, using as her textbook Prof. G. H. Bell's *Natural Methods in English.* Nearly the whole school met in the sawmill loft where she taught reading. Here chapel exercises and Sabbath meetings were also held. For a reading text, we used the Bible, articles from *The Review and Herald* and *The Youth's Instructor*, *Hymns and Tunes*, *Pilgrim's Progress*, and choice selected poems. The surrounding villages provided a laboratory for those who wished to gain an experience in giving Bible studies and conducting gospel services.

The larger number of students in attendance at the school that first year were mature young people who, after a brief preparation, entered some branch of gospel service. There were also a number of children in the school. Mrs. Lacey taught the primary grades. She must have been a good teacher, for 9-year-old Mabel, who for health reasons had not attended school beyond kindergarten, entered the Australian equivalent of fifth grade the following year.

Another first-grader who made remarkable progress under Mrs. Lacey's tutelage was Robert Hare, son of Metcalf Hare, the business manager. Robert later became a physician and was for many years connected with the Washington Sanitarium and Hospital, nineteen years as medical director.

A recitation hall and other buildings were soon added to the school plant, and a neat, commodious church was erected, with two large wings that were used as Sabbath school classrooms. On special occasions they could be opened to enlarge the main auditorium. Elder and Mrs. Haskell taught the Bible classes and trained students in evangelism.

Gifts of money came in from abroad and capable workmen made valuable contributions of labor. Within three months of the time the decision was made to build a church, it was completed, free of debt. Those were the days when people "helped every one his neighbour," and all were willing to give a helping hand whenever possible without thought of compensation.

In the meantime appeals continued to come to Grandma from homes far and near, wherever there was illness. Miss McEnterfer was always ready to answer such calls. If they came by night she would saddle the riding horse and accompany the messenger to the home of the sick one; if in the daytime, Grandma would sometimes go with her in the carriage. At one such home Miss McEnterfer found an 8-year-old boy who had a deep cut in his ankle. While driving a calf out of the yard, he had stepped in a hole into which broken glass had been thrown. Lard had been applied to the cut and the foot bound up with a rag. After a few days it had become so swollen and painful that the boy's father took him twenty-three miles by train to a physician in Newcastle.

The doctor dressed the wound, gave the father a bottle of medicine to administer internally, and told him to apply bread-and-milk poultices, but he failed to tell him how to make the poultices. The foot grew worse and blood poisoning developed in the entire leg. The parents feared they would have to take the boy back to the doctor, who had intimated that it might be necessary to amputate in order to save the child's life.

Then the father heard about Mrs. White and the Battle Creek nurse who lived with her and immediately sent an appeal for help. When Miss McEnterfer reached the house, she found the wound black and showing signs of gangrene. The little fellow had cried day and night for a week. Sara administered hot and cold fomentations continuously for the first two hours, and by the time the wound was dressed the patient was fast asleep.

The next morning when Miss McEnterfer called at the home, she found the mother in bed with a new baby and the aunt who had attempted to carry out the nurse's instructions incapacitated. The woman had slipped with a kettle of boiling water in her hand and burned her leg and foot so badly that she could scarcely move. Now the nurse had two patients instead of one.

Bundling them into the carriage she brought them to Grandma's home. But her front room was occupied with overnight guests so the patients were brought to our house and beds made for them in Father's study. Water was kept boiling on the kitchen stove, and the boy's leg was treated every two or three hours. Besides fomentations and leg baths, charcoal poultices were applied to the wound at night. One morning when the poultice was removed, a piece of glass about the size of a grain of wheat was found in the dressing. After ten days' care, the patients were taken home to astonish their neighbors with their accounts of the remarkable cures accomplished "just with hot and cold water and charcoal."

Grandma never accepted payment for such services. After that experience, calls for help came on so frequently that Miss McEnterfer could not answer them all. Mrs. Rodd, a Seventh-day Adventist sister who was a practical nurse, gave a helping hand. She also directed students in the nursing class at the school. They were glad not only to be of service but also to gain practical experience in caring for the sick, many of whom were cared for in Grandma's home.

"The Lord is in these things," wrote Grandma at the time. "He is preparing the way before us for the entrance of truth. This is real medical missionary work. We shall take every case that comes, even if we have to make a hospital of our home."

This seemed an almost impossible situation. Each of Grandma's helpers had her typewriter in her own bedroom, because there was no other space available for offices or workrooms. Grandma began to talk of the need for a hosptial building where the sick could be cared for and instruction given in healthful living, and where students might gain nursing experience.

She sent appeals for funds to our churches in America and to the believers throughout Australia; but she said that no money was to be solicited from the poor people who lived in and around Cooranbong.

One day classes at the school were dismissed and nearly the entire Adventist community joined teachers and students in a combination picnic and workbee for the clearing of a twenty-acre plot of woodland donated by the school board to the hospital enterprise. The day turned out to be rainy, but work went on between showers. When a particularly heavy downpour came on, we went inside the church, which was close by, and had a praise meeting. Grandma spoke words of encouragement, and Father told stories of pioneer days in America and Europe.

A twenty-five-bed hospital building was erected. Flower and vegetable gardens were set out, providing the patients with opportunity for physical therapy. Before the building was completed, applications began coming in from sick people. Although charges were low some were not able to pay them. To my knowledge, however, no one was ever refused help because he was too poor to pay.

So the years slipped by. Our school in the wilderness flourished. But the time came when Grandma felt it imperative for her to return to the United States. In 1901 there was to be a General Conference session in Battle Creek, and she knew that vital principles were at stake. So on August 29, 1900 she left Australia, and her entire family of helpers returned with her to her homeland.

Launching Out on My Own

Our good ship, the *Moana*, anchored in the San Francisco Bay on Thursday night, September 20. All day Friday we were held at the quarantine station on Angel Island and it was not until very late that afternoon that we were allowed to leave. Some of Father's good friends met our group at the San Francisco dock and took us to their homes for the night.

One would have thought that Grandma would be exhausted after the long voyage, but the very next day, on Sabbath afternoon, she spoke to a large congregation in the Oakland church.

On the ship Grandma had wondered where her next home would be. But she did not worry about it, because, as she later wrote: "When I was on the vessel crossing the Pacific, on the way from Australia to America, the angel of the Lord said to me, 'I have a refuge for you.'" [1]

After landing in San Francisco she and Father began searching for this refuge. Father suggested she go up to St. Helena to the Sanitarium, and she journeyed the sixty-five miles. In hills and woods away from the city she found rest. Best of all, she found the "refuge" promised her by the angel. She wrote how it happened:

"At the Retreat [St. Helena Sanitarium] I was telling Mrs. Ings how thankful I was for such pleasant rooms. . . . I told her my experience in house hunting in Oakland. . . . Sister Ings then told me that there was a place . . . which she thought would suit me, and she wanted me to go and see it. . . . I went to see it, and found a place of retirement, on high ground, all ready for us to occupy." [2] "Here was a house all furnished, and we could, as soon as the decision was made and terms accepted, go into this house, and find everything ready in excellent order. . . . Here were horses, carriages, and nearly everything . . . in good order for us to possess. . . . I never anticipated so much in a home that meets my taste and my desires so perfectly. Next week we shall live in our new home and we will seek to make it a home after the symbol of heaven." [3] Besides the home and grounds, the Elmshaven Estate contained seventeen acres of fruit trees, three acres of pasture, two acres of garden, ten acres for hay, plus five acres of hilly land where a large spring was located. In the family orchard near the house were apple, pear, peach, cherry, plum, nectarine, fig, walnut, and olive trees. The prune orchard alone contained two thousand trees. There was also a large vineyard. The barn could stable six horses and at least two cows. This was the home God had indicated would be in readiness for Grandma. Here she could gather her workers together and without delay continue the preparation of her books.

The purchase was made, Grandma and her family moved in, and soon the click of typewriters could be heard coming from a four-room cottage between the house and the barn. This little house had been the home of the former farm manager and his wife. It could answer the immediate purpose until a more commodious office could be erected.

Father rented an apartment from a family living nearby. Mabel attended school, and I seized the first opportunity to travel over the hills to Healdsburg College, thirty-seven miles away. Our summer vacations were spent gathering and drying fruit on Grandma's farm.

One summer, under the delusion that distant fields are greener, Mabel and I went with friends to pick and dry fruit in the orchards in the vicinity of Vacaville. Unfortunately, there were more workers than jobs that summer and we went home nearly as poor as we started out. But I needed money for my next year's schooling. Why didn't Grandma help? I wondered. She did later, but that year there were demands upon her resources more urgent than our needs. So I hunted up my old bicycle and with a prospectus in hand, set out for Napa. From house to house I went, selling *The Desire of Ages*, *Steps to Christ*, and *The House We Live In*. After canvassing from Monday till Friday afternoon, I would pedal the twenty miles from Napa to St. Helena and spend the weekends at home.

One Friday afternoon, feeling unusually weary, I decided to make the trip by electric interurban car and bring my cousin, May Jones, home with me for a visit. By the time we reached St. Helena Station, I was feeling faint and ill, almost too weak to get out of the cars and into the buggy that was waiting for me. By Sabbath morning I was well covered with suspicious-looking spots. Mother looked me over carefully.

"It can't be measles," she said. "You've had both kinds of measles, and they say you can only have them once."

She took a second look. "It must be smallpox!" she exclaimed, backing away. The doctor who was called confirmed her diagnosis. He had read in the newspaper that there were three hundred cases of smallpox in Napa. I was placed in quarantine, and Mabel and cousin, May, were shut up with me because they also had been exposed.

Following the physician's counsel, we were fed principally on oranges, grapes, and other acid and semiacid fruit. Within a few days I was feeling normal. May had only a light attack and Mabel did not stay in bed at all, but spent most of the time outdoors in the sunshine.

Our confidence in the smallpox diagnosis was somewhat weakened when we learned that the epidemic in Napa had been so light that it was called "Manila fever." Not until years later, when repeated vaccinations failed to affect either Mabel or me, was the smallpox diagnosis confirmed. Ever afterward we were able to care for genuine smallpox patients without fear of contracting the disease.

One especially pleasant experience I remember of my early life in California was attending the Camp of Peace, a three-week teachers' institute held in tents on the side of Howell Mountain near the sanitarium. Frequent messages on the subject of Christian education had come to our church leaders through the Spirit of Prophecy. Schools must be established, textbooks were required, and experienced teachers were needed to prepare them. Earnest, prayerful study was given to this project at the institute, which was attended by some of our most prominent educators.

At its close, before the tents were taken down, several of the most progressive teachers in attendance were hard at work outlining courses of study and planning textbooks on the various subjects assigned them. I volunteered to teach the first four grades if I could work with an experienced person. But demands for church school teachers far exceeded the number of teachers available, and I allowed myself to be persuaded to accept an eight-grade school in Reno, Nevada. Today I stand amazed at my courage in taking on such an assignment!

There was insufficient time for the writing and printing of the complete church school textbooks before the opening of school in the fall. But the newly-appointed textbook writers did the best they could, preparing the lessons piecemeal in pamphlet form and sending them out month by month through the mail to the teachers.

One afternoon soon after the opening of school, I found my mailbox jammed with lesson pamphlets. By the time I had given them a cursory examination, it was long after midnight. Each pamphlet contained an entire months' lessons on a certain subject for a certain grade. I marveled at the skill with which the lessons had been prepared in so short a time. If only I had had time to become knowledgeable about the various subjects before trying to teach them, all would have been well. In the morning I took the materials to school and was obliged to begin teaching from them without having time even to read them through.

A few days later, more lesson pamphlets dealing with other subjects came along. All but one of the eight grades was represented in my school of twenty-three pupils, and in spite of my efforts to combine classes, I still had forty-two lesson periods listed on the daily program. I much prefer to draw a curtain over my first attempt at teaching. I might mention, however, that one of my pupils years later accosted my husband with the statement, "You know, your wife she learned me grammar, and I thought she done fine!"

Those lesson pamphlets marked the beginning of a concerted effort by early Adventist teachers to prepare textbooks for our church schools. Those dedicated, faith-filled pioneer teachers refused to be discouraged, and continued working, praying, studying, and counseling until finally, with the help of new recruits, they developed the symmetrical, practical, even glorious pattern of Christian education followed by Seventh-day Adventist schools today.

---

[1] Letter 14, 1911.
[2] Letter 133, 1900.
[3] Manuscript 96, 1900.

An Excellent Young Man

One Sunday morning a few weeks before the close of the school year, as I was busy writing lesson plans for the coming week, there came a knock on my door. I opened it to the woman in whose house I was living.

"Miss White, there's a young man downstairs who says he wants to see you."

"To see me? Are you sure he wants to see me?" I asked, although I had a pretty good idea who it might be.

"Yes, ma'am. He is asking for you."

Pushing my books aside, I glanced hurriedly into the mirror to see that I was presentable, then went downstairs to the living room to greet a rather expected, very special friend. Dores Robinson had come from St. Helena by train and had arrived in Reno a little past midnight.

"Well, Dores, I'm happy to see you," I said, extending my hand for his usual hearty shake. "I've been half expecting you since receiving that last letter you wrote."

"Yes," he replied with a smile. "For a long time I've been looking forward to having a good visit with you."

"Well, now is our chance, Dores," I said happily. Somehow I felt that this was going to be a very important day in my life.

Since we didn't want to be interrupted by chance callers or be seen together by my school children, who were ever eager for new topics of conversation, I suggested a walk out into the country. Dores agreed. "Get your hat and coat and we'll be off."

It was a bright, sunny day, but the breeze from the Sierra Nevada Mountains to the west was a little too cool for comfort, so Dores suggested that we might find a place at his hotel where we could visit. We went there and settled down in a corner of the lobby to reminisce and talk. It was an ideal spot, and we enjoyed our isolation among strangers passing in and out, and were ourselves entirely oblivious to the chatter and laughter all around us. I told him a story, one that I had reserved for just such an occasion as this, about the time when I had caught my first glimpse of him.

One Friday afternoon while we were still in Australia, Mother and I had been cleaning house, getting ready for Sabbath. "Ella," she said, "we are going to have company tomorrow. Elder and Mrs. Robinson, who will be teaching in the school next year, are coming to have dinner with us, along with their son. They say that he is an excellent young man."

On Sabbath morning I had gone as usual with a group of students who paddled a rowboat four miles down Dora Creek to hold Sabbath school and church services in a fisherman's cottage. Afterward we returned upstream to the boat landing, and I walked home through the woods. Arriving at our house, I discovered that dinner was in progress. Softly tiptoeing into the kitchen, I peeked through the pass-cupboard between the kitchen and dining room. Sure enough! The Robinsons were there, seated with our family at the table, and beside my empty chair sat the "excellent young man"!

Panic seized me. I grabbed a book and headed for the woods. There, seated on a log, I tried to read. But, not finding the book of any particular interest, I closed it and permitted my thoughts to wander. My meditations were of short duration. A "laughing Jack," perched on an overhanging branch let out a boisterous "Ha! Ha! Ha!" I shouted indignantly at the feathered intruder, but he continued his hilarious mockery—"Ha! Ha! Ha! Ha!"—until a handful of pebbles drove him off.

Suddenly it dawned on me that I rightfully deserved to be laughed at, running away like that from an excellent young man, and I past 17. Picking up my book, I hurried home, only to find the house deserted, the guests departed, and my family with them. I was left alone to ponder the foolishness of my actions.

It was nearly a year before I again saw the young man, and then for only a few brief months, when he was a member of Grandma's office staff at Sunnyside. Now, here we were together on the opposite side of the world.

At my request, Dores reviewed his recent years, going back to 1897, when he had begun medical school in Aberdeen, Scotland, on money lent him by a physician, one of his father's friends. But the long, winter nights spent studying in poorly lighted rooms, combined with many hours bending over a microscope, had brought on severe eyestrain and frequent headaches. His parents, who by this time had settled in Australia, heard of his health problem and sent him a ticket to Melbourne, where he might continue his medical course under more favorable circumstances.

It was while pursuing his studies there that he had received a testimony from Sister White, warning him that if he continued to attend medical school, instead of doctoring others he himself would need to be doctored. Her advice was that he give up the study of medicine. Dores was greatly disappointed, because he had set his heart on following the medical profession. Yet he accepted the message as coming from the Lord, and joined Mrs. White's staff as a stenographer and typist.

Was it not divine providence that brought him and me together under so many varied circumstances? Dores asked.

Why was it that the only vacant space around the entire premises in which he could set up a typewriter had been my father's office in our cottage across the road? And why was that little office the only room in the house where I could escape the boisterous play of my gleeful twin brothers and do my studying for school? Dores remembered that often he had stopped the clicking of his machine to help me master some intricate problem.

I remembered that at such times I had found in him just the help I needed. Why, he could name all the bones in the human body, explain the operations of the nerves and muscles, and figure as rapidly in English money as I could in American currency. Also during his college days he had been a member of the debating society.

So, while I had struggled with my assignments in physiology, accounting, and rhetoric, and he typed away on the manuscript for the forthcoming book, *Christ's Object Lessons*, we had become good friends.

Still looking backward while sitting in that Reno hotel lobby, we recalled our Sabbath afternoon "sings" around the organ, to which the young people of the neighborhood had been invited, and our Friday evening walks through the woods to attend missionary meetings at

Avondale College. We talked on and on of these delightful experiences.

Dores had seen us off at the station when we left Australia for California. At that time, as he and I parted at the little station near Cooranbong, he handed me his photograph with the request that I return the favor. This I had done, and a correspondence followed, which strengthened our friendship through the next three years of separation.

After we left Australia, Dores found work helping to build the Sydney Sanitarium. This enabled him to act on the counsel Grandma had given him regarding his need for "more vigorous physical exercise." Later, he crossed the Pacific and went to Battle Creek, hoping to find employment at the Sanitarium. He became secretary to Dr. David Paulson, still hoping to earn enough to pay off his longstanding debt to his father's friend. But the salary was so small that he decided he would have to try some other plan. He therefore entered the colporteur work, as it was called then, handling Dr. Kellogg's medical books.

Dores' chosen field of labor was Montana. Arriving there he discovered that towns were far apart and most of them not large. Unable to afford any better means of transportation, he purchased a bicycle and began traveling from town to town and from farm to farm. Working in this fashion in rain and cold, he contracted rheumatic fever. A kind Adventist sister took him into her home and cared for him for many weeks until he was able to travel again.

Although the colporteur work had not been a tremendous success, Dores had discovered that he could give Bible studies and bring people to a decision for Christ. All his life, Dores Robinson was to be a soul winner. After recovering from his long illness, he agreed to teach a church school. This was a new and valuable experience for him.

Meanwhile, back at Elmshaven the office force was unable to cope with tasks awaiting their attention. Grandma continued to write voluminously. Realizing that more help was needed, Father remembered the excellent service Dores had given during the final months of our stay in Australia. He wrote, inviting him to join the Elmshaven staff.

The letter arrived in Montana toward the close of the school year. Since this seemed to Dores to be a move in the right direction, he accepted.

When he arrived, I was studying at Healdsburg College. We saw each other on my occasional weekend visits home and during summer vacation.

Now, taking advantage of a slight pause in our reminiscing, Dores spoke abruptly and to the point.

"Ella, I am sure that you can guess why I came all the way from St. Helena to see you. Remember the promise you made me the day you left home to teach in Reno? You said you would fulfill it under one condition: that I wait for you first to achieve your ambition of becoming a fully established, qualified church school teacher. You said you thought this would take about seven years and then asked half in fun if I would be willing to wait that long. I told you, also jokingly, that I could surely do no better than follow Jacob's example. But I have been wondering whether it is still your irrevocable decision to insist on that plan."

As he slipped his arm around me and his eyes looked into mine, I knew that the great moment had come. There in that hotel lobby, we settled the question. With a little gentle persuasion, I agreed to shorten the waiting period from seven years to one. That weighty question settled, our mutual promises were made, which we sealed with a fervent kiss—our first.

In the gathering dusk I walked with him to the station and saw him board the train. You may be sure I needed no one to wish me pleasant dreams that night, and I have often wondered what I taught my pupils the next day.

School closed a few weeks later and I returned home to find the family in deep perplexity. The time for Father and Grandma to leave for the 1905 General Conference session had arrived. Ordinarily Sara McEnterfer would accompany Grandma to this important gathering, but this year she found it impossible to go. Grandma greatly desired my stepmother to take Sara's place and accompany her, but this posed a problem. How could Mother leave the 7-year-old twins and 5-year-old Grace and the boarders in her home? It was Dores who came up with the perfect solution.

"If you can persuade Ella, we will get married immediately and stay here and take care of the home and the children while you go to the conference."

Ella was persuaded, and so the wedding date was set ahead one year.

Looking back now, I am truly thankful that we did not miss even one of the fifty-two precious years we were to spend together.

Setting Up Housekeeping

Our friends planned a pretty wedding for Dores and me on Grandma's lawn. But at the last minute a rainstorm blew up and we had to hurry to the sanitarium chapel and leave our decorations behind. However, it was a memorable wedding. Father performed the ceremony and Grandma gave an inspirational talk. Among other things she said:

"God wants the home to be the happiest place on earth, the very symbol of the home in heaven. . . . Marriage does not lessen their [the couple's] usefulness, but strengthens it. They may make that married life a ministry to win souls to Christ. . . . As the family relation is formed here below, it is to give demonstration of what they shall be, the family in heaven above. The glory of God is ever to be made first. . . .

"I would say, Make God your Counselor. Blend, blend together. . . . Let the light of heaven shine right in the home . . . in every word and in every action. You are not called to give up your identity. . . . Well, then, how shall they blend? Counsel together. And if there be any difference of opinion, yet we would say, Counsel together, and the blessing of God will come right into the heart."*

Her prayer, which followed immediately, included not only the bride and groom but the entire audience, the sanitarium family, the church, and all of God's children.

The following evening a serenading party found me at the ironing board helping Mother prepare for the trip to Washington. She was upstairs packing. Father and Dores were at the office, gathering documents and materials to be taken to the General Conference. Our honeymoon came several weeks later when Mother returned with the others from the East and resumed her responsibilities in the home. Dores and I then accompanied Grandma on a three-week tour, visiting the three newly acquired sanitariums at Loma Linda, Glendale, and Paradise Valley, in southern California.

Seventh-day Adventists had been instructed that it was their privilege to demonstrate God's love by means of ministry to the needy and suffering. But how could our members do this? They possessed little of this world's wealth. The purchase of these three sanitariums, at about one third the original cost of erection and equipping, made possible a forward move in medical missionary operations throughout our ranks. By frequently recounting God's special providences in times of crisis, Grandma gave new impetus to the work and fresh courage to the workers.

In after years, she often visited these sanitariums and gave counsel and encouragement to those connected with them. Loma Linda was her special delight. She foretold for it an important future, not only as a sanitarium but also as an educational center in which medical missionaries were to be educated for worldwide service. Of this institution she said, "I am thankful that we have a school at Loma Linda."

My father's home, which we called the White House, was near Elmshaven. It stood on a knoll between the health-food factory and the main traveled road leading from St. Helena up the steep mountainside to the sanitarium. In that beautiful little valley surrounded by pine-covered hills, we found many peaceful places to walk, and many delightful meals were served to invited friends under the pine trees in our own yard. Among papers of long ago there has been preserved the menu of a Thanksgiving dinner served around the long picnic table, which on this particular occasion seated twenty-one. The usual items generally listed on an orthodox Seventh-day Adventist Thanksgiving menu were all there, as well as the names of those present and where they were born. Reading this list indicates that we were truly a cosmopolitan group. The host, my father, was born in Rochester, New York, and his wife, May, our stepmother, in Calcutta, India. The twins and Grace first saw the light of day in Cooranbong, Australia, and their two younger brothers, Arthur and Francis, in St. Helena, California.

Professor Krasof, whose family had an apartment in our house, began life in Kiev, Russia, and Mrs. Krasof in Athens, Greece. Mr. and Mrs. B. Johnson came from the United States; Mr. A. Carter was born in Cambridge, England, and his wife in Geelong, Victoria, Australia.

Mrs. Perillat and daughter, Phyllis; Prof. W. B. Netherton and wife; Janie Workman, and our distinguished guest, Elder Arthur G. Daniells, president of the General Conference represented widely separated points in the United States. Dores and I began life about as far apart as was possible on this continent, he hailing from Washington, New Hampshire, and I from Oakland, California.

Grandma White was not present. In her older years she seldom attended such functions, but lived quietly in her peaceful home, Elmshaven. Thus preserving her strength, she poured it forth in her ministry of writing and speaking.

On her birthday, November 26, Grandmother rose early, as usual, and helped the family harvest the crop of Japanese persimmons. The orchard yielded three bushel baskets that year, and she picked until the last of the luscious fruit had been gathered. Later in the day Professor Hill, teacher of the local church school, brought the children to sing for her. Grandma was seated on the front veranda, and after the songs she visited with the children for half an hour.

Father reminded her that it had been sixty-five years since the family physician allotted to her only three more months of life. Since that day she had labored in human weakness but in divine strength as it was given her day by day, always sufficient to meet the needs of the hour.

Having made the overland train trip from Michigan to California shortly after the transcontinental railway line was opened, Grandma had since made countless similar crossings. She had spoken to hundreds of large audiences to which many individuals came simply out of curiosity to hear a woman preach. They had gone away thrilled with a new understanding of the plan of salvation and a new appreciation of God's eternal, unchanging love.

Father also reminded Grandmother of her two and one-half years spent in Europe, and her long journeys on that continent. She had labored for nine years in Australia, building up our gospel and institutional work in that country. The circulation of her books had reached an impressive figure, and she had definite plans for writing yet more. Many of her books had been translated into foreign languages and were being circulated throughout the world. When questioned how all this was made possible, she gave all the glory to God. The

Thanksgiving season was truly meaningful for her.

One day when the twins were about 14 years old they received a notice to the effect that a freight shipment was awaiting them at the St. Helena station. To their joy and delight, when they opened the large box they found a printing press with equipment and several fonts of type.

This was a gift from Uncle Edson, Father's older brother who was working in Tennessee. The type was some that he no longer needed in his printing business, but it was still clear and usable. Although the press had been badly damaged in transit, the twins became inspired to get into the printing business at once and felt there was no time for delay. Father was away in the East, but with Mother's consent, they paid the freight charges and took the broken press to the blacksmith's shop for repairs.

The well-meant gift from their Uncle proved unsatisfactory, but Grandma, realizing that this could be the beginning of something good for the boys, enlisted Mr. Clarence Crisler to purchase a little press and some basic printing equipment in San Francisco. The cost was $125. Before long the twins were able to notify the sanitarium, the health-food factory, the residents of the community, and the businessmen of St. Helena that Henry and Herbert White were ready to receive orders for job printing. From then on, their time was divided between school, printing, and gardening, with heavy emphasis on the printing. They transformed the old prune shed on Grandma's farm into the Elmshaven Press. As their work expanded, Father and Grandma bought new type and equipment for them, and the twins had all the work they could keep up with and still do justice to their studies.

As a young man, Father had worked in the Pacific Press printing office. At that time he regarded a knowledge of typesetting as an essential part of every young man's education. He had arranged for the twins to obtain a little printing experience while they were still in elementary school.

When Henry and Herbert got into the work, they found that they had to develop their own practical business skills without Father's help, for he was often away from home just when they needed him most. At such times they could often be heard singing as they went about their work, "Oh, where is our wandering Pa tonight?"

When college days came, the press was transferred to Angwin and became the College Press. It provided work for many ambitious students who needed to earn as much of their school expenses as possible. Besides operating the press, the twins taught printing at the college. Later in China, Herbert was to superintend the Signs Publishing House for six years.

In the meantime my husband and I had settled down in a small apartment in Father's large house, fully expecting to remain there as long as Dores was needed in the Elmshaven office.

Teaching in Chico

Dores and I had been married less than a year when Prof. E. D. Sharpe, educational secretary for the California Conference, came to visit us. One of the church-school teachers had resigned, and he was searching for a replacement. Would I come and finish out the year in this emergency? The very existence of the school was at stake.

When the problem was presented to Grandma, a wave of incredulity swept over her face, and she exclaimed, "What? Ella teach a ten-grade school all by herself? I think you had better go with her, Dores."

At this time Grandma was writing steadily on her books, so was traveling and preaching less than in previous years. That meant fewer sermons to record—certainly not more than Mrs. Maggie Hare Bree could handle, she reasoned. Grandma said she could spare Dores for the few months that remained before the close of the school year.

So Dores and I went off to Chico to teach church school. Father was in the East. When he heard what had happened he was dismayed. He was fully aware of Grandma's deep sympathy and concern for educational work. But he also felt that her work at this time demanded a larger rather than a smaller staff. Tasks were piling up—copying, duplicating, filing, indexing—enough to keep Dores busy for a long time. My husband was also the chief reporter of Grandmother's sermons and interviews. But by the time Father's objections reached Elmshaven we were already in Chico. In fact, we had agreed to stay for the following term.

The former teacher had used the church auditorium for his classroom. Now, since we were dividing the children, we had to divide the teaching space. This we did by stretching a curtain through the center of the room.

On one side I taught the first four grades. I had twenty-three children; Dores taught the sixth, eighth, ninth, and tenth grades on the other side. He had twelve students, mostly big boys. He had already been warned that these boys were unruly and that this was what had discouraged their former teacher.

As might be expected, my students were easier than his to handle, though the older students presented no great problems. All my pupils were lusty singers, but no complaint was ever heard from the class on the opposite side of the curtain. The church members were very cooperative. When school supplies were needed, the good-natured school-board members dipped into their own pockets. Nor did Dores and I ever go hungry while waiting for our monthly check.

About the beginning of the new year, our pastor C. N. Martin, began a series of Bible lectures in the church. Every day at the close of school the older boys would stack the school desks and chairs against the wall and bring out the benches, ready for the evening service. After the meeting the benches would be removed and the school desks and seats set back in place.

On the second or third day of school a student, Cecil Urquhart, asked my husband to consider conducting a class in bookkeeping. He was confident that if he could only get his brother, Edward, into the school, he would be converted, and bookkeeping was the only subject in which Ed was interested. Could Professor Robinson offer that subject as an inducement for him to attend?

Dores asked for a day to think it over. That afternoon the two school-teacher staff held a prayer and consultation meeting.

"Ella," Dores said, "I've never had a day's instruction in bookkeeping, nor do I remember ever talking to a bookkeeper about his profession or ever opening a book on the subject. But how can I evade such an opportunity as this to win a soul for Christ?" There could be only one answer.

My husband sent for a set of lessons and books, then sat up nights studying them. Bookkeeping was one of the subjects taught in the Chico church school that semester. Dores always felt that the results justified the effort, for Ed Urquhart was converted, went on to gain further education in our schools, and finally sailed for Korea, where he and his wife spent most of their lives laboring as devoted and much-loved missionaries.

About five o'clock one spring morning Dores and I were awakened by a vigorous shaking that lasted the best part of a minute, but which seemed like hours. It was April 18, 1906, the day of the San Francisco earthquake and fire.

We dressed quickly and hurried out into the street. The post office was not far from where we were staying. By the time we reached it, we could see that it was already open and filled with people who were anxious to get in touch with friends and relatives living in the earthquake zone. The line for the telegraph window stretched for more than a block.

A month later we two weary teachers mounted our bicycles and cycled the 120 miles back to Elmshaven and the office with its ever-waiting work. Father freely forgave us for running away, subject to our promise not to do it again.

That Chico church school was to prove one of the most productive in the denomination in terms of workers sent to foreign fields. Besides Edward and Maud Urquhart, there were other well-known missionaries who came out of that little school. These included Merritt and Wilma Warren, Alfonso and Mayte Anderson, Charles and Fred Landis, Chloe Landis, and Harry and Irene Parker. Altogether some forty-four candidates for foreign mission service obtained at least a portion of their education in the Chico church school.

We were glad, and so were Father and Grandma, that we had met the emergency and not allowed that school to be closed. We felt assured that God had divinely directed us in making our decision.

Finances

After our return from Chico, Dores and I took an apartment on the second floor of Father's house, where we continued the pleasant association with our family and where I could help now and then with the routine work at the office. It was there, in the White House as we jokingly called it, that our first child, Virgil Eugene, was born early in 1908.

As we now had two Grandma Whites—Great-grandma Ellen G. and Grandma Ethel May—the latter suggested that to save confusion we call her Mamma White. She didn't like being called Grandma, anyway, as it made her feel old, when in reality she was still a young woman.

Ellen G. White had given Father a few acres of land near her home on which he built a house and planted an orchard and garden. The adults living there soon became aware of the fact that there were two babies in the house, our own Virgil Eugene and Mother's little Arthur Lacey White, who preceded Virgil by three months. The two boys became great playmates and spent much time together as long as we lived near Elmshaven.

Finances were really nip and tuck, with all of us stretching the pennies. Clothes were worn as long as there was any wear in them and then cut down for younger members of the family.

Once when Elder A. G. Daniells was visiting in our home, he playfully turned our 3-year-old son over his knee, pretending to spank him. Noticing that one leg of his trousers was a slightly darker gray than the other, he looked up at me quizzically and I hurried to explain.

Mother had cut down a well-worn pair of Father's trousers into a pair for Henry, and a pair of my husband's, also well-worn, for Herbert. When the twins had gotten all the wear possible out of them, they were handed on to me. From the usable portions of both outfits I salvaged one last pair for our little son. Henry's trousers were slightly darker than

Herbert's; and that's how it came about that one leg of Virgil's was slightly darker than the other. Elder Daniells laughed heartily when he understood the situation.

Our parents had built a large house, hoping that by renting apartments and taking in boarders they might extend the influence of a Christian home to young people who were working in the nearby health food factory, and at the same time recover the cost of building the big house. Another reason was to have room available for renters so that Mother and the children would not be left entirely alone during Father's many and long absences.

We knew that generous-hearted Grandmother White would gladly have increased the salaries of her workers were it not for the continually advancing expenses incurred in connection with preparing the manuscripts and getting out her new books, a task she was pushing forward before her lifework should close. In those days our publishing houses were not in a financial position to meet all the expenses of producing the books called for, and often the cost of illustrating, typesetting, and plate making were borne by the author. This was the case with such books as *The Ministry of Healing*, *The Great Controversy*, and *The Acts of the Apostles*. The author, who had advanced the money, would recover his investment by way of a royalty, a certain percentage of the sale price of each book sold.

The translation and abridgment of books for overseas mission presses was an expensive proposition, and Grandma bore much of the burden. The heavy costs not only consumed her resources, but called for the borrowing of money. Besides these demands upon Grandma, appeals were constantly coming to her for financial assistance in establishing schools, health institutions, and printing offices overseas. At the same time, she always felt a personal responsibility in caring for sick and discouraged workers, and in assisting promising but impoverished youth to gain an education.

Grandma could not bear to see the publication of much-needed books delayed; she would at times mortgage her book royalties far into the future to keep the wheels moving. The workers in her office shared her self-sacrificing spirit and were willing to accept a small wage, even if it meant going without some pleasures and, at times, even some things that were usually regarded as essentials.

After Dores and I had been married five years we began thinking about building a home of our own. Between Elmshaven and Father's house were two acres of tillable land that Grandma gave to Dores and me for a building site. Here we erected a five-room cottage complete with basement and sleeping porch.

Our new home was completed three months before our eagerly awaited daughter made her appearance. On that hectic night, only one hour before her arrival, Dores' parents, Mr. and Mrs. A. T. Robinson, and their teen-aged daughter, Gladys, were on their way from the St. Helena station to our home. They had come from Nebraska for a long-anticipated, long-promised visit. They were met in St. Helena by Father White's carriage and taken to his home, where they were cordially entertained and treated to supper, baths, and beds. Dores, torn between anxiety over what was happening at our house and a natural desire to visit with his parents, whom he had not seen for several years, moved nervously back and forth between the two houses.

Next morning the Robinsons, who had been informed of the arrival of their first granddaughter, walked down the hill to our cottage. They ohed and ahed over the new baby in proper grandparental fashion, counted her fingers and toes, observed the color of hair and eyes, discussed that most difficult question of which of her ancestors did she most closely resemble, and finally pronounced her "a perfect child," a fact that her parents knew already. We named her Mabel after my sister.

During the Robinsons' three-day stay, they were entertained at the "White House," and we also enjoyed many delightful visits together while I lay cuddling my little one. Then Father Robinson had to return to his duties as president of the Nebraska Conference. Gladys remained with us for several months, and she and I formed a close attachment that continued through the years.

The spring after building our cottage we planted some fruit trees and made a strawberry patch and a kitchen garden. Then we decided to go into the poultry business, with the hope that in time it would help reimburse us for our expense in building our home. We planted an alfalfa patch, fenced off a chicken run, and built a poultry house.

Unfortunately, Dores and I were both inexperienced at this

business. To our disappointment, the project increased rather than diminished our financial obligations. Many a night after the children were asleep we sat together at our kitchen table studying our budget. The interest on our house mortgage was absorbing too large a portion of our income.

Fortunately, we managed to avoid discussing our financial problems in front of the children. They never realized that we were poor, except perhaps when they found it hopeless to linger over the toy counters in the stores we infrequently visited in St. Helena.

To show how successful we were in maintaining a worry-free home atmosphere, I will incorporate here some memories Virgil has written covering his early years.

"We had a small plot of ground beside our house, part of which was planted to strawberries. We used to go out regularly with Mother to pick them. When there was an extra nice lot, she would pick a couple of baskets and have me take them over to Elmshaven for Grandma White. Of course, I did not usually see her, for she was up in her room, busy with her writing; but the housekeeper would take them and thank me. Occasionally we would see her pass in her carriage while going for a drive with Miss Sara McEnterfer, her nurse and private secretary; and sometimes, by previous arrangement, Mabel and I were permitted to go riding with them.

"Sometimes we visited the fruit orchard and gleaned some fruit for our table. For our playground, we had the whole world of nature. Oh, those were wonderful days as with my companions I roamed the fields and hills surrounding Elmshaven.

"The big barn was a wonderful place to explore and in which to play. There were stalls for the horses, and one corner had long rows of hens' nests. The best fun of all was to climb the ladder into the hayloft, where we could run and jump and tumble with the utmost abandon. What fun it was to watch the hay being thrust down the big holes into the mangers for the horses! And what wonderful lanterns that barn had. Real bull's eyes they were, with globes much thicker and larger than ordinary lanterns and much more expensive. One of these had been left hanging under the bridge that spanned the creek, where repair work was being done. I must have been about 4 years old when one day I picked up a stone and threw it at the lantern. Crash! It was a straight shot, but I think Father was rather sorry he had spent so much time teaching me to throw straight at tin cans set up in our back yard. Before I got through with that episode, I was as sorry as he. Those globes were rather costly.

"Above the sanitarium, about a mile from our home, I had a number of playmates. On the main road to the college lived the three Walter children—Edwin, Marvin, and June. Their father ran the general store at the sanitarium. Coming home one day from a visit to the Walter children on the hill, I stopped at the store to look around. I was inspecting a box of fig bars when the clerk asked me if I wanted it. I nodded my head. He handed it over and asked if there was anything else. In a few moments my arms were full of all kinds of sweets and cookies. I had made a wonderful discovery: you could get anything you wanted at the store by just saying, 'Charge it.' I shared my goodies with all the children I met and arrived home blissful over my wonderful discovery. I do not remember how Mother went about impressing me that everything in life has to be paid for by someone, sometime, but I am sure she did!"

Mother Lifts the Mortgage

"I [Virgil] did not know that the building of our house had cost more than was planned. Father's small salary barely covered the ordinary household expenses, to say nothing of liquidating the debt on our house. Any suggestion that he leave his work as one of Mrs. White's secretaries and find more remunerative employment was never for a moment entertained by any of us.

"For several years when the trees leafed out in the spring and the birds began to sing, Mother would harness our black horse, Babe, to the one-seated carriage and journey to other communities to sell Adventist books and, at times, aluminum cooking utensils. Finding her best customers living far off the beaten track, she frequently headed for the foothills of the Sierra Nevada Mountains. For four summers and one winter she continued this work until the debt on our house was greatly reduced. From her earnings we also arranged to have a modest cottage built on Howell Mountain, near Pacific Union College. Here Mother hoped at some future time to live and educate her family, and incidentally, to finish her own schooling. But most of the time it was rented to others. (Years later the cottage was to burn to the ground only five weeks after its insurance policy lapsed.)

"Mother's selling trips were not without their dangers. Many of the miners were rough men and Mother did a lot of praying as she went into unknown country. One day she knocked on the door of a decrepit shanty and was greeted by a strange-looking individual who guided her to a room lighted only by one small candle, and then disappeared."

(Here I take over from Virgil):

I looked around. In the far corner of the room I saw, sitting in a chair, what appeared to be a skin-covered skeleton. To my great relief, it spoke.

"Were you looking for Nellie? She won't be here tonight."

I started to explain the object of my call.

"Don't get the things out, dearie; I couldn't see them if you did."

The voice coming from that eerie figure was that of an old woman, whom I later learned was 103 years old. She was totally blind and so stiffened with arthritis that she seldom moved from her chair. The huge man sitting in another corner was her grandson. He apparently gave her the care necessary to keep her alive.

I left the old woman with some very brief, very important remarks. "When Jesus lived here among men, He healed all the sick and gave sight to the blind. He has promised to come again and take away all pain and suffering and to give us new bodies that will never feel old or worn out or weak."

"Yes, dearie, I know," she said with a sigh as I backed out of the room. Babe and I went on our way.

Once while canvassing in the foothills of the Sierras, I came to a village without a single inhabitant. Windows were boarded up and the forlorn cottages were surrounded by weeds that seemed more like small trees. I knew Babe was hungry, and, remembering the apple and shredded-wheat biscuit that I carried for my emergency lunch, I was too. But, there was no suitable place to stop and eat. It all seemed so weird. I drove on, but there was no sign of life anywhere.

Then, what a relief! Half a mile past the village, we came to a neat cottage, and a little fox terrier ran out to the front gate wagging his tail and barking a friendly greeting. The visit with the lonely woman living there was refreshing to us both. Faithful Babe seemed to appreciate the extra feed she received that day, and didn't leave one kernel of grain in her nose bag.

While I ate my lunch and drank the glass of cool milk my kind hostess poured for me, she told me the story of the deserted village. It had once been a prosperous hydraulic mining town. The process of washing gold from the soil rapidly filled up the valley. A farmer would buy a piece of fertile land, plant an orchard, garden, and alfalfa field, and build a house and barn. After a few years his trees would be half-buried under a fresh layer of soil washed down from the mine above, and he would face the prospect of using a second-story window instead of his front door as the entrance to his house. The valley people appealed to the local government, and a stop was put to the hydraulic mining in that vicinity. This decision, however, came too late. Within a few weeks, the entire population had moved away and were looking for places elsewhere to settle, leaving the village deserted.

Life in the mining towns of California during the early part of the century was rough. I know that my guardian angel protected me on more than one occasion, and perhaps on many others when I was not conscious of any danger. It was a wonderful feeling to know that I was God's child, and that my heavenly Father was caring for me.

The Curtain Falls

Life was pleasant in our own home in Pratt Valley, only a couple of hundred yards from Grandma's comfortable Elmshaven residence. It was a pleasure to go into our strawberry patch while the dew was still sparkling on the grass and leaves and pick a panful for breakfast, stopping now and then to pop a particularly luscious jewel into my mouth.

Adjoining the berries and safely secured behind a stout fence, we planted alfalfa. How our Jersey cow enjoyed feeding there! Each morning and evening Dores would bring in a foaming pail of milk so rich it was almost golden yellow. Since we had been warned of the danger of bloating that threatened cows permitted to eat wet alfalfa, we carefully kept Bossy in her stall until the sun had dried all the moisture on the field. But one morning she managed to sneak into the patch, and by the time my husband went to milk her, she had gorged herself on the tempting green food.

We knew at once that we were in trouble. Even as we watched, we could see her sides swelling and soon she was bellowing in agony. It was hard for her to stand, yet she could not lie down. Dores remembered that a friend had once told him that a quick cure for bloating was a dose of kerosene. We simply couldn't afford to lose our only cow; she represented far too large an investment.

Into a tin can we poured a pint of kerosene. Then while Dores held her head and managed to open her mouth, I poured the oil down her throat.

The result was astonishing. Within fifteen minutes the cow that had looked like a gas balloon bore much more the appearance of a clothes rack, with every rib showing. Bossy was saved, but we couldn't drink her milk for many days. I think we might have burned it in the lantern, it was so impregnated with kerosene. We later learned that a tablespoon would have been ample. But at least we had saved our cow.

While traveling from house to house with Babe and the buggy in the rough mining towns of California, I had often been impressed by the thought that after delivering my orders, I would probably never see those people again. Sometimes I would carry a stack of *Signs of the Times* with me and leave one at each house. But I often wished I had something I could leave that would last longer than the papers. I could not afford to give the larger books away, but the thought came to me that one of the Adventist publishing houses might be willing to print a book carrying a timely message that would take the light into the homes of my customers and to hundreds of thousands of other isolated families.

This desire became so strong that in the fall of 1914 I wrote to Elder Palmer, manager of the Review and Herald Publishing Association. Ever since Mabel and I had traveled from California to Australia in the care of Elder and Mrs. Palmer we had regarded them as special friends, and I felt free to contact him now.

World War I had broken out only a few months previously. Men and women everywhere were thinking more seriously than ever before about world events. Would it be possible, I asked Elder Palmer, for the Review and Herald Publishing House to print a 100-page paperback book dealing with the current world crisis and selling for not more than twenty-five cents?

Although I had hoped that the idea would receive favorable consideration, I was unprepared for Elder Palmer's enthusiastic reply. He had shared my letter with the book editor, and together they had decided that here was a workable idea. They next blocked out ten topics to which they gave chapter titles. Since it would take too long for one person to write the book, they allocated different chapters to writers of ability on the staffs of the Review and Herald and the General Conference.

The work was going forward rapidly, Elder Palmer assured me, and the book would be out by Christmas. Delighted with the prospect of having something to take to my customers, I promptly ordered two hundred copies. Early in December I found the following announcement on the back page of the Review:

The World's Crisis
In the Light of Prophecy
(*Ready December 15*)

The following is the outline of subjects:

"Light for Our Time in the Prophetic Word."
"The European Conflict: Is It Armageddon?"
"Approaching Armageddon."
"Turkey and the War." . . .
"Christ's Second Coming." . . .
"The Home of the Saved."

This book will contain about 128 pages, with paper covers in two colors. . . . Price, 25 cents. One hundred copies by freight, $12.50. On an order of 200 copies the freight will be paid.

A hundred thousand copies should be sold this winter.

Thus was born the plan whereby millions of copies of inexpensive World Crisis Books would be scattered throughout the world.

The year 1915 came, a year that would bring great changes in our lives. February found Virgil, Mabel, and me in Grass Valley. A friend took the children back to St. Helena while I remained to complete my selling.

On May 28 I arrived in St. Helena on the morning train. Dores met me and we drove home, both happy to know that my trip was ended. That afternoon I disposed of my prospectus and the aluminum-ware sample case, feeling that I should never need them again. I never had further use for the sample case, but years later, in South Africa, I had the joy of selling many hundreds of copies of *The Great Controversy*, *The Hope of the World*, and *Our Day in the Light of Prophecy*. At heart, it seemed, I would always be a colporteur!

On February 13, Grandma, now 87, had tripped and fallen heavily while going to her room. Cousin May Walling, her nurse, had rushed to help her but found that any movement caused severe pain. A doctor was called, and after a brief examination she was taken to the sanitarium, where an X-ray revealed a fractured femur. There was no treatment for this type of injury in those days, so Grandma was returned to Elmshaven, where she was confined to her bed. Fortunately, she did not have to endure much suffering, but what pain she had was borne without a murmur.

Friends from near and far came to see her. Soon after her accident, she expressed the opinion that she felt her lifework was done. She did not anticipate being able to work again. Yet her faith, hope, and confidence seemed to grow stronger as the days passed.

The work at the Elmshaven office continued. It had been three or four years since Dores, on his morning walk to the office, had stopped at Grandma's room to collect the ten, fifteen, or twenty pages of handwritten material to be taken to the office and typed out. But the work of book preparation continued as her staff brought her materials together for such books as *The Acts of the Apostles*, *Prophets and Kings*, *Counsels to Parents and Teachers*, and *Gospel Workers*. Grandma participated in this, reading chapters, writing in corrections, and adding some new material.

Ever since Grandma first met Dores in Australia she had taken a keen interest in him and his career. While she prized his literary work in her office, she was also eager for him to engage in public ministry. She rejoiced when he took an active part in pastoring the St. Helena and Calistoga churches and in conducting Sabbath afternoon services for the disabled and retired soldiers in the Yountville Veterans Home. She had heartily approved of his ordination in 1910. Now she felt the time had come for him to labor in some community where there was no Seventh-day Adventist church.

With grandmother's illness, work at the office was carried on at a slower pace, so Dores wrote to the president of the California Conference offering his services. As a result, it was arranged for us to go to Willits and cooperate with Elder Andrew Nelson in holding a tent effort, with the youthful C. Lester Bond as song leader and tentmaster.

On the last day of June, 1915, Dores and I and our children slipped into Grandma's room to bid her goodbye. Somehow we knew, and she knew also, that this would be the last time we would see her alive, and we cried a bit together. She blessed her great-grandchildren and we had prayer; then we walked quietly down the stairs and out to the carriage waiting to take us to the station, where we boarded the train.

Upon our arrival in Willits Elder Nelson met us and took us two blocks to the lot where the big tent had been pitched. At first we wondered whether there would be room for another family tent, but in the end we managed it, and our three families settled down.

As the days passed, the meetings at the tent continued to draw a fair number of people. For me the most important moment of the day came when the postman walked up to our tent and handed us the morning mail. Nearly every day there was a letter from Father, telling of Grandma's gradually weakening condition. Also, every week we eagerly scanned the back pages of the *Review* for the note Father had written concerning Grandma's condition. When we read the words "What a strange world this will be for me when Mother is gone," there were a few moments of tears. Ever since the death of his father, James White, Papa had been Grandma's constant companion and helper.

When church members everywhere read Elder White's report of his mother's condition in the *Review and Herald*, they realized that she would not live much longer:

"The following, dated at Sanitarium, Cal., July 2, will be of interest to all our readers: 'There has been no decided change in mother's condition during the past two weeks. She gradually grows weaker, and for five or six days has seldom spoken above a whisper. Today she said to me that she was thankful that the Lord continues His mercies; and a little later, in broken sentences, she expressed her confidence and trust. After I had prayed with her, and spoken of the glad day when Christ will make all things new and we shall meet our dear ones around His throne, she expressed her hope that the time would not be long. Last Sunday morning she was feeling a little better than for several days, and Elder and Mrs. G. B. Starr came in to bid her good-by. When they expressed pleasure at finding her so bright, she said: "I am glad you find me thus. I have not had many mournful days. The Lord has arranged and led in all these things for me, and I am trusting Him. He knows when it will end." At times, she expresses a desire to rest, and seems to feel that the day of rest is near at hand.' "—W. C. White, *The Review and Herald,* July 15, 1915.

The next day Ellen White died.

On Friday afternoon, July 16, as we were preparing the tent for Sabbath, a Western Union telegraph boy rode up on his bicycle and handed Dores the telegram we had been expecting. With trembling hands he tore open the envelope and read Father's brief message: "Mother fell asleep at 3:40 today. Funeral Sunday."

The next morning we boarded the train for St. Helena. Father was there to meet us with the carriage, and we drove to the house that had been our home for four happy years.

On that Sunday afternoon, crowds of people came to the funeral service, which was held on the lawn in front of Elmshaven. Elders J. N. Loughborough, G. B. Starr, and Eugene Farnsworth, pioneer workers with whom Grandmother had been associated for many years, were there to take part in the service.

Monday we went by train to Oakland, where a second funeral was held at the California Conference camp meeting in nearby Richmond. Elders E. E. Andross and E. W. Farnsworth led out. The family occupied seats in the front row, where we could watch hundreds of grieving friends file past the casket. When they had left, we too gathered for one last look at the calm, peaceful face of one whom we had loved so dearly.

We then drove to the railway station, where we said goodbye to Father and Sara McEnterfer as they boarded a train that would carry them, and Grandma, back to Battle Creek. After a third funeral in the Tabernacle, she was laid to rest by the side of her husband, two sons, and other family members in Oak Hill Cemetery.

Grandma's passing marked the end of an era for us. Standing there on the platform in Richmond station, we could not help wondering what the future might hold. Tomorrow we would return to Willits and continue our meetings at the tent until the evangelistic effort should close. But what lay beyond that?

Could we have drawn the curtain aside, we would have seen us move to Colorado the following spring, followed by two years of preaching and teaching in that field. There followed a term in Nashville, where Dores joined the editorial staff of the Southern Publishing Association. In 1920 our family sailed across the Atlantic to do mission work in Africa. There, in Capetown, our third child, Gladys, was born. Some seven years later, back in the United States Dores was invited to join the White Publications office, working there and in Washington for twenty-four years, until his retirement.

Little did I know that, like Grandma, I too would lose my companion and have to walk alone after fifty-two years of most rewarding companionship.

Soon, very soon, the heavens will part and the Saviour will come. God's sleeping saints shall hear His voice calling them to life. Graves in every land scattered over this wide world will open. The ocean depths will give forth their treasure, and "many shall come from the east and west, and shall sit down . . . in the kingdom of heaven" (Matt. 8:11).

Loved ones parted amid heartache and tears shall meet and "never, never part again."

* * * * *

Ella May Robinson lived for ninety-five and one-half years, dying in 1977.* It was in her eighty-ninth year that she typed out this manuscript. Her last letter was to her children—Virgil in Africa; Gladys, the youngest, in Iran; and Mabel, living nearby. We feel certain that Ella would wish to include in this her last message everyone who has read this book. She wrote:

"It looks as if I shall not last many days longer. I think I am nearing the end. Oh, I have so much to praise the Lord for. How can we realize how blest we are in being able to work for Him to the end of life? We may stumble when the path is rough, but let it never discourage us.

"The darker the night, the closer we press to His side. The rougher the path, the firmer we hold His hand, and we press on, singing as we journey. We see the glory streaming down the golden streets through the open gates and we raise a richer song of praise.

"Meet you just over the hills in the land where joy shall be forever, Mother."

* Note: The publishers requested Arthur L. White, Ella's younger half-brother, to read the manuscript critically. Having worked in the Ellen G. White Estate since 1929 and currently engaged in writing a multiple-volume biography of Ellen G. White, his appraisal that the manuscript is remarkably accurate in its detailed depictions is significant and gratifying. In a few instances he has made minor corrections in the interest of accuracy, as has Ella's son Virgil.—Editor.